PAAT PAANI

Preeti Deo

Publishing facilitation: AuthorsUpFront

To my late mother-in-law,
whom we'll keep alive in our
memories carrying on her
legacy from generation to
generation.

Contents

Foreword

I met Preeti on Facebook while I was in the process of releasing my film Shank's, centred around Marathi food, in the UK. I received a message from her saying how thrilled she was after watching the trailer, and how she was looking forward to watching the movie. We shared some messages, and then I realized that she was the one who had made all of the recipes from the Marathi cookbook, *Ruchira*, in the UK. I remembered reading about her in newspapers. I was amazed. *Ruchira* is an iconic cookbook which every Marathi household in the world has, but the book has always been considered a reference manual. However, Preeti made it her textbook and followed every recipe as it was written by Late Kamalabai Ogale, and actually made each and every *padarth* (delicacy) from the book in spite of living away from India. What tremendous passion! I knew I had found the Shashank I had made up for my film.

Then on, we kept talking – about food, about Marathi cuisine, about her journey of making 300-plus recipes. Her stories were thoroughly inspiring. How she managed to get each and every ingredient mentioned in *Ruchira* in the UK, how she walked miles in the snow to get something as rare as *maaeen-mula*! Along with her extremely supportive husband Rajesh and son Pranav, she had arranged an event to commemorate the culmination of her cooking journey. They graciously invited Gautam (co-screenwriter and co-editor of *Shank's*) and I to be part of the event virtually, and our families just became part of their family from then on. I still remember that my wife Madhura and Preeti – one in the US and one in the UK – coincidently made semolina cake on the same day, and we had a good laugh about how telepathy works with food.

This book is Preeti's personal journey through the different facets of Marathi cuisine. Everything, from bread to desserts, from baking to roasting to frying, has a special place in her childhood. The book doesn't only mention about recipes, but also about family practices revolving around Marathi food in general. Her discourses about *pangat*, a thorough description of *phodani* (tempering), its procedure and reason for adding it to food, her remembrances of *maadi* in her house and her comparison of it to Alice in Wonderland… everything is a great joy to read. There are so many books and videos about recipes, but this is a book about a cuisine where culture, practices and recipes form a great bond.

Marathi food is very much ingrained in our minds, therefore there are a lot of things we tend to take for granted. One of the very important messages I got from this book was we should step back for a moment and just have a broader look at the wealth of knowledge our ancestors produced in the past. The answer to almost every question we could possibly have is hidden there. All we need to do is pull the curtain aside and discover it.

My very best wishes to Preeti and may this book bring a great awareness of the Marathi cuisine in the world.

Ashay Dileep Javadekar
Director, *SHANK'S*
40 Ayrshire St Bear DE 19701
+1-302-229-3937
www.ashayjavadekar.com
www.njemovies.com

Author's note

Paat Paani is about my journey in the kitchen learning the nuances of family recipes associated with Marathi cuisine. It is written with the intention to showcase regionally-focussed Marathwada cuisine from the Western part of India.

This is my first book, and it is almost impossible to convey the emotions that a first-time author experiences. The project has flooded me with an exhilarating sense of accomplishment. I hope this book, which is written in a natural, conversational style, will be accessible to those who are new to cooking traditional regional cuisine, especially from Marathwada. I have included nostalgic memories of food, family traditions and treasured recipes that I believe will help break down the tricky aspects of this little-known culinary style, and help make it accessible. My friend and incredibly talented artist Sunita Khedekar has drawn beautiful illustrations of the ladies in my family who have inspired me to cook.

Growing up, I recall the holiday meals cooked by my aunts. I remember the ladies gathering in the kitchen to cook under *Ajji's* watchful eye. Everyone contributed to the meal preparation. At times I was asked to fetch a lime or a twig of curry leaves from the backyard; other times I would sit down with my siblings and cousins to churn buttermilk, peel boiled potatoes or clean coriander for garnishing. I always wanted to feel important like the ladies standing by the stove, and would plead with my grandmother to allow me to be a part of some main cooking activity. *Ajji* would take the opportunity to make me feel special and declare me the official in charge of setting the table, along with the clan of kids in the house. Once the mini jobs that we were assigned were done, I would happily organise my team of siblings and cousins to gear up for *paat paani*, which is Marathi for 'setting the meal table'. The boys were assigned to arrange the colourful *paat*, low wooden stools to sit on, while the girls collected the *taat, vaatya, pele* and *taambya* to arrange in front of each *paat*. The next task, one that the girls enjoyed most, was to adorn the *pangat* (row of seats from which to savour the meal) with *rangoli, or colourful designs on the floor*, while the boys filled each *tambya* with water. Just when we thought we had accomplished what we had set out to do, and were all set to announce it, we would hear Ajji's voice reminding us that "*Rangoli var halad-kunku ghalayla visru naka ga porinno...*" (Girl, don't forget to dot the rangoli with turmeric and vermillion). Dotting the rangoli with these two coloured powders is considered auspicious. Someone would grab the *kunka chi koiree* (a paisley-shaped container, usually made of brass or silver, used to hold vermilion and turmeric) from the *devghar* (in-house temple) and sprinkle *its contents* on the patterns we had created. Everything was done creatively and rewarded with an extra helping of *Saaran* (filling) made either for *Karanji* or *Modak* or even *Puran*. I guess we did not have reward charts back then, but such gestures would motivate us to carry on the task throughout the vacation. I would happily wait for Ajji's signal: "*Porinno, paat paani ghya ga...*" (Girls, please set the table). *Paat paani* makes me nostalgic, thus the book title.

This book has happened because of so many kind souls. In no particular order, I express my gratitude to them…

I am grateful for the role I have at work, which has taught me to love myself and find happiness in the smallest of things around me. Working in a Special Needs Department, where each day is different and challenging, is one of the most rewarding jobs I have ever had. In order to calm my mind after work and to relax, I generated interest in cooking.

Rajesh, my husband and my best friend, knew that this book was my dream and soon made it his goal too. He stepped into the kitchen very often to allow me the time I needed to write.

Pranav, my son, who enjoys cooking and eating as much his father and I do, has chipped in with suggestions and the motivation I get from him has always been valuable.

Vasant Deo, my father-in-law and Rajesh, helped translate the book into Marathi and I can't wait to see that version.

Meenal Bhave went through the manuscript to proofread it. I recall sharing my desire to write for the first time with Manjiri Gokhale Joshi author of Bosses of the Wild, Chef Manoj Vasaikar from Indian Zing, London, and Chef Asma Said Khan from Darjeeling Express, London. They trusted my decision. I would also like to thank my foodie friends Kaumudi Marathe, Kalyan Karmakar and Saee Koranne-Khandekar for their timely advice; Anjali Koli, Sharmila, Amit and Minal Sangekar, Kedar-Anuja Deshpande and Priya Deshingkar for moral support and for being such lovely buddies. Also Ashay Javdekar for his continuous support in this journey and for kindly writing the Book foreword to avoid reusing the word for.

My parents Govind and Shobhana Patki, brother Kaustubh and his wife Veronica my sister Shruti and my brother-in-law Parthesh Gulawani for brainstorming on titles and Trupti Joshi, Dipti Modani, Umesh-Arundhati Deo, Shyam Degloorkar and all my cousins for believing in the manuscript. Rajesh and I have spoken endlessly to each one of them on the phone to find out more about the women in the family who contributed to keeping family traditions alive, and for the recipes cooked every day and on special occasions. I am incredibly grateful to the contributors to this book – the late Ujjwala Deo, my mother-in-law, Shobhana, my mother, Sheela Yermalkar, my maternal grandmother, Gangabai Patki, my paternal grandmother, my great mothers-in-law the late Laxmibai Deo, and Vimal Degloorkar, my sister Shruti Gulawani, my aunts Vijaya Itolikar, Saroja Kulkarni, Sudha Pade, Pratibha Kulkarni, Pushpa Deshmukh, Sushila Deo, Smita Joshi, Radhika Yermalkar and Sangeeta Degloorkar, my sister-in-law Arundhati Deo, my niece Aishwarya Deo, my cousins, Shilpa Kulkarni and Anuya Kulkarni,

Shruti Degloorkar and her extremely talented mother, Aparna Kulkarni. Last but not least, Manish Purohit of AuthorsUpfront, my editor, Ramya Sarma, and cover designer Neena Gupta for their time, assistance and pulling the final stage of the book together.

Thank you all for giving me this opportunity!

Lady and the milling stone

Introduction

Food Encounters

My earliest memory of food is my mother (*Aai*, in Marathi) cooking in our house in Durgapur, West Bengal.

I was born in Maharashtra and brought up in West Bengal. Growing up, I was oblivious to the various factors associated with the culinary styles of different regions – Bengali cuisine in West Bengal and Maharashtrian cuisine in my native state, Maharashtra. As a child, I was a fussy eater. Aai made futile attempts to feed me with a variety of food preparations. I ran away from vegetables and dals. Aai would have to find clever ways of camouflaging these, or stuffing them in the flat breads called *Polya*.

I relished *Polya* spread with a generous helping of *tup*, or clarified butter, and sugar. My mother makes the thinnest and softest *Polya* in the family. At times, a roll made with jam or condensed milk spread liberally would satisfy me, because I have always had a sweet tooth. On the savoury side, I preferred *Varan-Bhaat-Tup* (plain rice with boiled lentils and clarified butter) or *Metkut-Bhaat*. Metkut is an amazing mix of selected spices added to a variety of lentil powders.

When we moved to the City of Joy, Kolkata – Calcutta, as it was called then – it was great experiencing the local delicacies and the quintessentially Bengali sweetmeats like mishti doi, or sweetened yogurt, and roshogolla, Indian cottage cheese balls served in sugar syrup). I could eat the sweetmeats at any time and in any quantity. Bengali feasts at our family friends' home or even at weddings was when I relished the most intriguing flavours and textures.

My blue school bus would pick me up from Gol Park. With the traffic, the bus would take a good hour just to reach Darga Road. It was a fun, foodie ride to and from school. All the girls, including me, had a stash of goodies packed in our bags, which we would tuck into with gusto. The memory of sharing school lunches with my school friends is fresh even today. Our best moment was at the end of the day. The jhalmuriwallahs always stood outside the school at the end of the day. Just as the buses drove slowly through the school gates, we would hastily fling our arms out of the window to purchase Jhaalmuri (puffed rice flavoured with chaat masala). At times, the bus darwaanji (conductor) would step out to help buy the snack for the whole busload of children!

I had an appetite for such street food. Phuchka (puffed, crisp puri filled with chickpeas and flavoured water), Egg Roll, Radha Vallabhi (lentil-stuffed puri)-you name it, and I could hog these endlessly! Understanding and developing a palate for Marathi food came significantly later in my life.

When we moved to Maharashtra, It was – fortunately – to the historical city of Kolhapur. My siblings and I went through a sudden transition in academics, culture and weather. Our young minds were coping with the changes in our lifestyles. *Dada*, our maternal grandfather, had accompanied us to help the family settle in to our new place. It was undoubtedly a different experience when we spoke in our mother tongue both inside and outside our house, unlike in Kolkata, where we talked multiple languages, including Marathi, Hindi, Bengali and English.

My palate was quickly acquiring the tastes of traditional cuisine in this part of Maharashtra. Be it the home ground spices and the variations of the *tambda rassa* (red stew) and *pandhra rassa* (white stew) or the vegetarian spread – including the *pithale*, gram flour cooked in tempered and seasoned stock made with sugarcane juice – the flavours have remained lodged in my mind until today. Much later, as I grew interested in the uncomplicated and rustic fare served every day, the emotions associated with food started becoming evident. I experienced food with a little more involvement.

Realisation

I moved to Pune for further studies and explored Marathi food, more than before. Our food mess served Marathi *dabba* (tiffin); my roommate and I shared a single *dabba* and that was more than sufficient for me. Gradually, we were turned off by the same old *bhaaji* (vegetables) and *daal* (lentils), in the dabba so we decided to eat at a *khaanaawal*, a small place that served homemade meals. Mavshi, who owned the *khaanaawal*, was a sweet lady and served us all with love and care. If she had made a snack or a dessert for her children, she would never forget to set aside some for us too. Her passion for cooking was reflected in her flavoursome meals from the coastal region of Maharashtra. *Rassaa Bhaaji* (vegetables with gravy), *Paale Bhaajya* (green vegetables), *Masaale Bhaat* (subtly spiced rice with vegetables), *Kadhi* (a thick soup based on gram flour flour) and *goadaache padaarth* (desserts) – we savoured them all, one by one. Mavshi was an incredibly chatty person. She would never fail to strike up a conversation at mealtime, usually about something of interest on the menu. I think her *Matkiche Kalan* (soup made of buttermilk, mustard seeds and coconut) was by far the most divine thing I have had in my life thus I recall these food moments so distinctly even today. I believe I started enjoying my food then and took greater pleasure in Aai's traditional spread on every visit home.

When I got married, I managed to observe the more subtle nuances of cooking and to serve meals in a fairly authentic manner. I always wanted to help, although I was afraid of making mistakes. So I watched – I noted how each meal was cooked and served judiciously, taking into account the left, right and centre part of the *taat* (plate). There was a set of rules and an order in which the traditional meal was served, with each course on a particular place on the plate. I was surprised how the ladies draped in nine-yard sarees would cook the multi-course meal with ease to serve the family of 50-70 people; but when I looked at the massive spread on the kitchen platform, I was apprehensive. I dreaded it even more because there was talk of the whole process being just not laborious, but complicated. This obviously posed a considerable problem for someone as inexperienced and uninitiated as myself. Unfortunately, since we moved to England, I had very little time to learn in this particular kitchen.

Had I encouraged myself to look at those problems and figure out how to solve them, it possibly would not have been as daunting. Today though, I would urge all beginners to give any complex technique and laborious dish at least one go. With strategies chalked out and an organised mind-set, each level of complexity can be ticked off to achieve the goal. It is indeed challenging, yet rewarding! Cooking is important, but should also be pleasurable. It is an imperative skill for anyone of any generation.

Motivation

I have always been naturally inclined towards crafts, painting or even dancing. Cooking somehow became a passion when I travelled far from my native land. I was not aware that this essential life skill would be my happy activity later in life. Since I was adamant about not learning how to cook, my mother felt frustrated, for sure. However, I believe that the assurance of her own experience would have told her that I couldn't go on for too long without entering the kitchen.

I took up the challenge to learn the basics of cooking through the iconic cookbook Ruchira, by the late Kamalabai Ogale. My experience in using Ruchira connected me with a woman who was creative, smart, persistent (her daughter's chat revealed that) and determined.

It was paramount for me to understand the original recipes, procure the right ingredients and find the time to make it work and, of course, await the right weather that the methods demanded, especially to make the pickles and *paapads* – the British climate posed a significant challenge! However, as I organised myself along with the temperamental English weather and worked through the methods, creating and presenting each dish was such a beautiful feeling of attainment. Slowly, as I started overcoming the challenges, cooking seemed very interesting and less daunting.

A decade ago, if anyone had asked me about food, my reply then would possibly have pointed towards a merely utilitarian purpose. Today, however, my perspective has changed. Cooking now helps me to express and communicate my feelings differently. Like a painting can convey a thousand words, just one taste can convey the gamut of enjoyment I experience in the kitchen.

Food blogging has connected me to the importance of food photography so well. Photographing my food made me appreciate it even more. The props, the colours, styling and processing added another feather to my gastronomic experience. I had never thought I would fall so head-over-heels in love with cooking and food photography. It was interesting to realise how the same *bhaaji* I served in a vessel – or at times in a *kadhai* – had a distinct appeal when plated with care and style. I enjoyed eating and my family enjoyed my cooking. Every meal served was being enjoyed. Personally, I realised that treating and respecting your food well is a symbiotic act. There is more pronounced nourishment with the time, love and care you put into cooking as well as eating.

As I began delving deeper into my understanding of food, it became clear that slow and patient cooking leads to beautiful flavours and textures. Marathi food uses a number of spices and knowing what the combinations are was imperative. Spice blends in certain proportions can enhance flavours, while an incorrect spice or one used in improper amounts can spoil a meal. It took me a while to understand the flavour of each of the spices and the right combination with which to enhance various preparations.

We see many talented chefs working towards presenting regional cuisines to conform to international standards. Marathi cuisine involves genuine techniques and resources to create a multi-course meal. I believe reinterpreting some of the recipes in a form that allows their characteristics to stay the same will help people from different communities to relish this cuisine equally as the other cuisines.

My quest now begins to bring to the fore similarities in the traditional cooking techniques of Marathi and other cuisines around the world, despite differences in culture, people and topography. Every region in the world has its special characteristics and methods of meal-making. A few dishes like pithle that we have share similarities with the French 'mother sauces' and few others are close to the Italian fresh or hand-rolled pasta. I was intrigued by aquafaba (the water in which beans have been boiled) in traditional *Kalan* and the fact that regional barbeques are part of the winter carte du jour. This comparability with Marathi cuisine makes it easier for my son and hopefully the next generation to accept it with a newer perspective.

There are common misconceptions about Indian food in the West. The most frequent I must mention is 'curry' and 'curry powder'. In fact, these terms have often been conversation starters. The moment I am introduced to a non-Indian, conversation steers towards curry.

It requires a good number of meetings and an invitation home for a meal, when I get the opportunity to show that Indian cuisine is vivid and rich. I manage to convince my guests about curry powder not being essential to Indian cooking and how the process involves blends of spices – sometimes negligible in the gravies for various sides of legumes and vegetables. For many in the West, the experience of Indian food is limited to the curry and naans that curry houses dish up. Educating the community in a new culinary vocabulary is necessary.

This book unfolds, one chapter at a time, with heaping helpings of food memories from the past. It also shows how I got over the apprehension of cooking in my English kitchen. The mise-en-place is conducive to the need to conserve the authenticity of the cooking techniques. The photographs and illustrations stand out as visual inspiration for readers. Each chapter has a story associated with the attributes of Marathi cuisine – I experienced this so well in my family.

I am what I tasted, observed, sensed, heard, read in the past and am still experimenting with in my kitchen in the UK. Myriad food memories have helped me stay connected to my roots. We all have strong recollections of someone cooking for us that linger. My visits to my grandparents in Aurangabad, Aai's kitchen and even my in-law's after my wedding are such beautiful evocations. Such reminiscences act as precursors to my everyday routine and make it better with every attempt.

PAAT PAANI

The recipes in the book are quick, handed down from my family, that I have tried curating for posterity. These family notes collected virtually at times and shared with reliable advice and wisdom from the past generations by my aunts and cousins at others are beyond methods, nutrition and calories.

Pickles and Preserves

With Gangabai Patki, Govind Patki and Shobhana Patki

Apricity

Winters in India mean perching on the window, soaking in the subtle warmth of the sun. With fresh vegetables and limes available in local markets during the season, this is the time of year when *Aai* is always busy. She spends most of her winter afternoons mixing pickles of all sorts. Her pickle cart includes jars of sweet and sour ones for the youngsters and the more piquant kind for the elders in the family. These pickles mature through the winter season in huge pots and make our favourite meal accompaniments for the rest of the year.

Having a jar of pickle ready to serve is a boon, especially when the meal planned is short of *Kaalvan*, other accompaniments like *bhaaji* or *varan*. A tiny serving of sapid pickle enhances the dynamics of a plate of plain *Poli-Bhaaji* (flatbread with vegetables) or even *Aamti-Bhaat* (lentils and rice). Traditionally served on the left side of a plate, pickles do not just enhance the taste of a meal, but their gastric help with digestion and overall good health of the gut.

Pickles and making them always reminds me of life in our quarters in the CMERI colony in Durgapur when *Tai* (my grandmother) came to stay with us. Clad in her soft *Ilkal* nine-yard sari, Tai kept herself warm with a green *Himroo* shawl wrapped around her shoulders as we sat in the backyard overlooking our vast garden. That shawl was testimony to *Tai's* life and food, with the faint aromas of sugar and spice and all things delicious that had been made while she was wearing it. Aai sat on a stripy *chatai* laid out on the veranda. She had a row of pickle jars ready to be filled, to last for the year. Tai, Baba and I watched her as we sat on our *baaz* (char-pai, or string cot). My little sister was to be born that month. Even today I can recall our family sitting on the veranda as *Baba* fiddled with his new toy, a camera he had bought in Stuttgart.

Ghol Limbu

My late mother-in-law spoke about her *sasubai* (mother-in-law), saying "*Aajjini maathat khade meeth ani limba ashich thevun, gholun kele hote lonche. Diwsa daha-bara vela. Maath potyavar thevun gholun thevun dyaychya.*" (*Ajji* placed the limes with rock salt in a clay pot. She would roll the container on a hessian cloth ten to twelve times during the day). I always admired the large *barni* (pickle jar) that held the last batch of this pickle that *ajji* made before she passed away. The limes were nowhere near green-yellow; they had darkened beyond recognition and they had softened which is the term my family refers it by *gal limbu*. The maturing of this medicinal pickle in salt gave it a typical, sharp taste, and I was lucky to have tasted *Ajji's* culinary skills in this traditional form.

My mother suggests adding crushed carom seeds and juice extracted from ginger, in her version of the pickle.

Ghol limbu is a whole lime pickle made by pricking the lime and adding coarse salt. Traditionally the pickle is made in an earthen pot and rolled on a hessian cloth every day. The friction between the salt and the limes draws the juices out of the citrus fruit and the pickle is ready to eat when the lime skin has softened and darkened.

Since I do not have access to an earthen pot, my pickle is matured in a regular glass jar. I tie a *daadra*, soft cloth over the jar and shake it every day so that the limes are pushed into new positions each time.

This pickle doesn't mandate any specific proportions of salt, shredded ginger and carom seeds. The whole mixture amalgamates into a tremendously medicinal concoction, and can be used to treat various digestive ailments. It even helps stimulate the appetite and build immunity.

This pickle is best eaten as a side, especially with a plate of piping hot *khichadi*, *paapad* and *saar*. A convalescing person can savour *ghol limbu* with a comforting bowl of *saadha varan* and *bhaat*.

. . . .

Hirvya Mirchiche Lonche

Ingredients

Green chillies 1 cup, chopped

Mustard powder 3 tbs

Salt 2 tbs and additional 1 tbs

Fenugreek powder 1/2 tbs

Turmeric 1 tbs

Lemon juice 1/2 cup

For the tempering
Oil 1/4 cup

Asafoetida 1/2 tsp

Mustard seeds 1 tsp

Method

Mix mustard powder, fenugreek powder, 2tbs salt together in a plate. Heat oil in a separate pan and temper with mustard seeds and asafoetida. Pour it the spice mix prepared in the plate. Let the mix cool. Add the chopped green chillies to the masala. Decant the pickle in a jar and top with the additional salt. Set aside. Pour lemon juice after a day and mix well.

Store in an air-tight jar.

Waalke/Gudmakai Lonche

Waalke or Gudmakai is a yellow-orange cucumber mainly great for favouring *aamti*, at times is added to *thaalipith* or even for pickling. I get this variety of cucumber often referred as Madras *kaakdi*, in many of the Asian stores in Wembley and Hounslow, selling South Indian grocery and vegetables.

To make the pickle, one needs:

Ingredients

Waalke/Gudmakai 1, cubed bite size

Crushed mustard 1 tsp

Lemon juice 1/4 cup

Red chilli powder 1 tsp

Turmeric 1 tsp

Fenugreek powder 1/2 tsp

Asafoetida 1/2 tsp

Salt to taste

Method

In a bowl, place the cubed *Waalke*. Add the dry ingredients to the bowl. Mix all the ingredients and add the lemon juice. Transfer to an airtight jar.

This pickle will last for a week in the refrigerator. We like this pickle as a side especially with *dahi-butti* (yogurt-rice tempered with green chillies and curry leaves) in summer.

Maeenmula Lonche

Maeenmula or Coleus roots have medicinal properties and are great when pickled.

Ingredients

Maeenmula 3-4 roots, washed cleaned

Mustard seeds 1 tbs

Fenugreek seeds 1 tsp

Turmeric 1 tsp

Red chilli powder 1 tsp

Salt to taste

Lemon juice 1/4 cup

For the tempering

Oil 1/4 cup

Mustard seeds 1 tsp

Asafoetida a generous pinch

Method

Grind the mustard and fenugreek seeds. Add turmeric, red chilli powder, asafoetida and salt. Set this masala aside.

Peel and chop *maeenmula* into small pieces and place in a bowl of water; this prevents the roots from turning brown.

Mix the masala, together with salt and lemon juice, making sure that the spices coat the pieces evenly.

Put the pickle into a jar.

Heat oil and temper with mustard seeds and asafoetida.

Let the oil cool and then pour it over the pickle and mix well.

Store in an air-tight container.

This pickle makes a great accompaniment with everyday meals, *thaalipith* or even an uncomplicated plate of rice and lentils.

Moraawala

This is a sweet preserve made using Indian gooseberry.

Ingredients

Indian gooseberries
(aawala) 1 cup, grated

Sugar 1 cup

Cardamom powder ½ tsp

Saffron 10-12 strands

Method

Wash the gooseberries and wipe dry.

Grate them and measure out 1 cup.

Mix the grated gooseberries and ½ cup sugar and set aside for a couple of hours.

In a separate vessel cook ½ cup sugar and ½ cup water. On a low flame till the sugar syrup is slightly more than one-thread consistency.

To the sugar syrup, add the grated awala. Cook till the grated aawala gains a translucent look.

To this mixture, add cardamom powder and saffron. Mix well.

Cool and store in an air-tight jar.

Note: Moraawala is best eaten as an immunity builder condiment. I love it on my toast at breakfast too.

Ambe Haladiche Lonche

Ambe halad(Curcuma Amda) or wild turmeric belongs to the curcuma family of rhizomes. It is highly effective as an analgesic and imparts an acrid taste to the pickle.

Ingredients

Raw Turmeric *(Oli Halad)* grated 1 cup

Mango Ginger *(Ambe Halad)* grated ½ cup

Ginger *(Ale)* grated ¼ cup

Mustard seeds 1 tbs

Fenugreek seeds 1 tsp

Turmeric 1 tsp

Red chilli powder 1 tsp

Salt to taste

Lemon juice ½ cup

For the tempering

Oil 1/4 cup

Mustard seeds 1 tsp

Asafoetida a generous pinch

Method

To make masala

Grind 1 tablespoon of mustard and 1 teaspoon of fenugreek seeds. Empty into a small bowl. Add turmeric, red chilli powder, asafoetida and salt. Mix well. Set this masala aside.

Mix the grated ginger, mango ginger and raw turmeric in a bowl; add the masala which was set aside, salt and lemon juice. Mix well.

Heat oil in a separate pan and temper with mustard seeds and asafoetida. Let the oil cool and then pour it over the pickle and mix well. Store in an air-tight jar.

This pickle is best eaten as a meal condiment. Serve it with piping hot *tikhat mithaachya purya* (puffed breads) or even the cooling *dahi butti*.

Bhokrache Lonche

Bhokra or Gumberries in English, make a unique pickle. At times they are mixed with grated mango for variation.

Ingredients

Bhokra 200 g

Small raw mango grated (optional) 1

Mustard seeds 1 tbs

Fenugreek seeds 1 tsp

Turmeric 1 tsp

Red chilli powder 1 tsp

Salt to taste

For the tempering

Oil 1/4 cup

Mustard seeds 1 tsp

Asafoetida a generous pinch

Method

To make masala

Grind 1 tablespoon of mustard and 1 teaspoon of fenugreek seeds. Empty into a small bowl. Add turmeric, red chilli powder, asafoetida and salt. Mix well. Set this masala aside.

Wash and clean the berries.

Wipe the berries dry and remove the seeds.

Move the berries into a clean and dry vessel.

Thoroughly mix the pickle masala with the berries.

Heat oil in a separate pan and temper with mustard seeds and asafoetida. Let the oil cool and then pour it over the pickle and mix well. Store in an air-tight jar and consume within 15 days.

Karle Lonche

This *kaarle* (bitter gourd) and other vegetables pickle is made in the lemon juice. The sharp, citrusy juice masks the bitter taste which the gourds otherwise impart on their own. Pushpa aatya lovingly packed a jar of this bitter gourd pickle with us on our visit back to UK.

Ingredients

Green chillies 50g

Cluster beans 50g

Bitter gourd 2, chopped

Grind mustard and fenugreek seeds

Lemon juice 1 cup

Mustard seeds 1 tbs

Fenugreek seeds 1 tsp

Turmeric 1 teaspoon

Red chilli powder 1 teaspoon

Salt to taste

For the tempering

Oil 1/4 cup

Mustard seeds 1 tsp

Asafoetida a generous pinch

Method

To make masala

Grind 1 tablespoon of mustard and 1 teaspoon of fenugreek seeds. Empty into a small bowl. Add turmeric, red chilli powder, asafoetida and salt. Mix well. Set this masala aside.

Wash and clean the vegetables.

Wipe the bitter gourds dry. Chop into roundels and remove the seeds.

Wipe the cluster beans dry, string and snap into smaller bits.

Move the vegetables into a clean and dry vessel.

Mix the pickle masala with the vegetables.

Mix lemon juice.

Heat oil in a separate pan and temper with mustard seeds and asafoetida. Let the oil cool and then pour it over the pickle and mix well. Store in an air-tight jar in a refrigerator and consume within 15 days.

Limbache Lonche

Ingredients

Limes 1 kg

Sugar 2 kg

Red chilli powder 250 g
(optional)

Salt ¼ kg

Method

Wash, dry and chop the limes into small pieces. Get rid of the seeds. In a large vessel, mix all the ingredients but sugar until each piece of lime is well coated. Transfer the mix into a sterile jar, taking care to wipe the mouth of the jar clean. Close and set aside to for a couple of days.

The limes soften in the time period. To this add sugar and mix well.

Sugar dissolves in the juice exuded by the chopped limes. Give this pickle a good stir in the jar every day, until no sugar crystals are visible. When stirring, please be aware that any moisture can spoil the pickle. Thus care should be taken to use a dry spoon whilst stirring and the jar lid should be sealed tight.

This pickle begins to mature once the sugar dissolves in the pickle mix. Sweet Lime pickle can be served when fasting with sabudana khichadi or bhagar.

Raiwale Limbache Lonche

Ingredients

Juice of one large lemon

Mustard seeds 1 tsp

Cumin seeds 1 tsp

Asafoetida 1/8 tsp

Red chilli powder 1 tsp

Salt to taste

Method

Heat oil in a small pan. Add mustard seeds and let them splutter. Add cumin seeds and asafoetida. Turn the heat off and add red chilli powder. Once the oil is cool, add the lemon juice and salt. Mix well and use this pickle to add spark to a meal.

. . . .

Limbachya Saaliche Lonche

Don't throw away lemon peels! That is what Aai says. Lemon has many beneficial properties, and the skin can be used in a pickle. Once you have used a few lemons in the kitchen, try making this pickle with the peels that you would normally throw away.

Ingredients

Lemon peel 1 cup, chopped

Green chillies 1/8 cup, chopped

Ginger 1/8 cup chopped

Salt 1/2 tbs

Sugar 1 tbs

Red chilli powder 1 tsp

Ground cumin 1 tsp

Method

Chop the lemon peel into tiny pieces. Add chopped green chillies, chopped ginger and salt. Transfer the mixture into an air-tight jar and set aside for a fortnight. After a fortnight, when the lemon peels and ginger soften in salt, add sugar, ground cumin and red chilli powder. Mix well.

Kairi Lonche

Ingredients

Chopped mango 1 cup

Jaggery 1 cup, grated

Tempering

Oil 1 tbs

Asafoetida ¼ tsp

Mustard seeds ½ tsp

Cumin seeds ½ tsp

Red chilli powder ½ tsp

Turmeric powder ½ tsp

Salt to taste

Method

In a bowl. Add turmeric, red chilli powder, cumin powder, and salt. To this add chopped mango pieces and jaggery. Mix all the ingredients together. Transfer the pickle to a dry, air-tight jar. It will be ready to eat in a couple of days.

Heat oil in a separate pan and temper with mustard seeds and asafoetida. Let the oil cool and then pour it over the pickle and mix well.

Note: You can avoid using jaggery in this pickle if do not wish to make a sweet mango pickle.

. . . .

Saakhar Amba

Ingredients

Raw mangoes peeled and grated 1 cup

Sugar 1 ½ cups

Cardamom powder ½ tsp

Saffron a few strands

Method

Wash the mangoes and wipe them dry.

Mix the grated mango and sugar thoroughly. Set aside for a couple of hours.

In a large pan, cook the mixture on a low flame till the sugar syrup is slightly thicker than a one-thread consistency. Add cardamom powder and saffron.

Mix well. Cool and store in an air-tight jar.

Vaalvan

Marathwada is drought-prone and the average rainfall there is 30 percent less than in the rest of the country; as a consequence, there is a shortage of fresh produce. Thus, during winter, when the weather is dry yet not too hot, green leafy vegetables including tender green gram leaves, fenugreek leaves, amaranth, Indian jujubes, and vegetables including cluster beans, carrots, bottle gourds, bitter gourds and ash gourd are sun dried and conserved for use later in the year. Sundried and dehydrated vegetables play a significant part in the kitchen inventory, along with pickles and paapad. Sun drying preserves nutrients and protects the food from bacteria and fungus by removing the moisture.

Vegetables like green chillies, okra or cluster beans are coated with buttermilk spiked with cumin powder, seasoning and sun-dried too. Fried, these make a delicious accompaniment to meals at any time of the year.

Traditionally, *Saandge*, or dried lentil nuggets are prepared before *Gudi Paadwa*. Interestingly, no *vaalvan* (drying of food) is done before the auspicious occasion, unless it is for *upaasache padaarth* (food eaten when fasting). I believe the reason for this custom is the weather. The spring season provides the perfect temperature and sunshine to dry these kitchen essentials outside.

Sun dried snacks like *Kharodya* are made by soaking and crushing *jwari* or *baajri* in water. The millet mix is later soaked in buttermilk overnight. The next day, it is cooked with water and salt until the mixture comes together. The mix is spooned into tiny bits on a plate and sun dried for a couple of days. Together with raw peanuts, *kharodya* make great munchies.

Saandge

Saandge/vade are soaked and ground lentil mixes that are sun dried in nugget form and used throughout the year. A *supari* or betel nut (symbolising Lord *Ganpati*) is ritually worshipped before beginning the process of making the vade. Women apply haldi-kunku (turmeric and vermillion) – to signify prosperity and long life – on the supari before the little lentil nuggets are set out in the sun to dry. Either one lentil or a mix of lentils can be used to make vade.

. . . .

Moogache Saandge

Ingredients

Split Moog Daal 1 cup

Green chillies 2-3

Garlic pods 2-3

Salt to taste

Method

Soak the daal overnight and then drain the water. Grind the daal coarsely with the green chillies and garlic pods, without using extra water. Add salt and mix well. Place small nuggets of the mixture on a plate or a plastic sheet. Leave this in the sun for a couple of days until dry.

For mixed daal saandge, a mix of *Harbaraa* daal, Moog daal and Udid daal is used. The proportion of *Harbaraa* daal to moog daal to udid daal should be 1:1/2:1/4.

Paapdya and Kurdaya

It is interesting how food can bring the community together. The rolling of *paapad* and the pressing of *kurdaya* at the onset of summer is a classic example of the community spirit associated with cooking in terms of Marathi cuisine. The women of the family and from the neighbourhood come together to carry out the sun drying of various kinds of *paapad* and *kurdaya* made from lentils and grains.

I experimented – successfully, I must say – with a few recipes in the limited sunshine in the town where I live in South-East England.

....

Taandalachya Paapdya

Ingredients

Rice 1 cup

Cumin seeds 1 tsp

Salt to taste

Method

Soak rice in water for three days, changing the water every day. On the 4th day, drain the water and spread the rice on a kitchen towel and let it dry. Once dry, grind it into a fine flour. Sieve to ensure a finer powder.

Make a batter, slightly thinner than pancake mix, using water and the rice flour it should spread evenly on a plate when rotated.

To the batter add cumin seeds and salt. Mix well.

In a large pan, heat water to boiling point. Spread a tablespoon of batter on a plate and turn the plate over the pan with boiling water, so that the batter faces down towards the liquid.

In about 3-4 mins the batter will be steamed enough.

Quickly place the plate batter side down in a large pan holding cold water.

Carefully release edges of the steamed paapdya from the plate using a sharp knife. As soon the sides are loosened, the entire paapdi will be free.

Lift it out of the water as soon as possible and place it on a cloth to dry – an old cotton bedsheet works well for this. When you are done, place the sheet in direct sunlight. The paapdya needs a couple of days to dry completely.

Store in an air-tight container. Fry in oil and serve with khichadi or regular meals.

Tips:

1. The water should be boiling for steam to be released on every paapdi made. Maintaining the water temperature is imperative.
2. The pan with cold water needs attention too. Change the water if it warms up with the heat from the just- steamed paapdya. If one can procure a stand with multiple plates to steam these, a batch of saal paapdya can be steamed at once. I do not have such stand thus I make use of plates at home.

Saabudana Papdya

Ingredients

Sago seeds 1 cup

Water 3 cups

Salt to taste

Method

Wash and soak sago seeds overnight. To soak the seeds you need to wash them and drain the excess water, leaving just enough to help the seeds plump up. The next day, heat water in a large pan. To this add salt and the soaked sago. Cook until the batter starts to thicken slightly and a skin begins developing on the surface. Let this batter cool slightly, and then spread spoonfuls into rounds on a plate or a plastic sheet. Dry these paapdya in the sun for a couple of days. Once dry, store in an air-tight container. These paapdya are served ideally when fasting. These are fried in clarified butter or peanuts oil.

. . . .

Kurdai

Ingredients

Wheat semolina 1 cup

Salt to taste

Water to soak semolina

Method

Soak semolina for three days. Drain and refresh the water every day, making sure not to lose the chik (sediment). On the fourth day, drain the water for the final time. Measure the volume of the chik. Add twice the quantity of fresh water. Season with salt and cook on a low flame, stirring continuously as the batter thickens. Once the mixture is a thick and glistening mass, turn the heat off and cover the pan to keep the kurdai dough warm until use. Using a special kurdai press, or chakali paatra, express the kurdai in heaps onto plates or plastic sheets. Dry these tangled nests of noodles for a couple of days in the sun. Store in an airtight container.

Smita Mavshi and Radhika Mami

Chutneys and more

Howrah Station to Aurangabad

Our train journeys from Kolkata to Aurangabad were always fascinating and created everlasting memories for us all. It took us two days to reach our destination. In these two days, we'd go through innumerable experiences that remain vivid images in my mind.

Aai would begin packing a week in advance. The clothes were washed and ironed by the local *istriwallah* (vendors who would iron clothes using an iron heated with coals). The domestic help was instructed well in advance: "Deshe jaachi, feere ashbo, onyo jaygaye kaaj dhoreesh na" or 'We are visiting our homeland, but we will be back, so don't look for another job'.

Aai also had the humongous job of cooking and packing the food that we could savour on the train, to last for two days. She had a stash of *tikhat mithaachya purya, dhapaate, dashmya* at times or rice tempered for *dahi butti*. She'd set yogurt in separate clean jar which would be set by the time we had our meal on board. A massive hold-all, a few smaller suitcases, a little *surai* (clay pot to hold drinking water) and a long drive through traffic to Howrah Station – the sight of the iconic Howrah Bridge made us squeal in excitement, because it marked the beginning of the journey to our grandparents' house. Nostalgia!

On the train, I preferred being on the top berth. For most of the journey, I'd spend time flipping through the comics that I'd pester Baba to pick up on the railway platforms that the train stopped at, or read the stock of Enid Blyton books I had brought with me.

Aurangabad was miles away from Kolkata and numerous exhilarating experiences dotted the length of the exciting train ride. The stations were a cacophony of so many different activities. The stalls had the local radio station playing Bollywood melodies, occasionally interrupted by an announcement from the Station Master's cabin about arrivals and departures. There was the buzz of passengers alighting and boarding trains, vendors selling tea, biscuits, fruits, newspapers and even toys. Mineral or bottled water was not easily available then, but we had our *surai* that Baba would top up whenever the train halted at a station. That was the only time I disliked being on a train. I had the fear of leaving behind Baba on the platform, just in case there was a long queue at the drinking water taps. What if the train left the station and he couldn't get on fast enough! I remember one time he got off to fill the pot and buy some snacks for us; there was a very long queue at the taps and there was no way he could fill the *surai* and buy food before the train left. My sister Shruti and I kept looking out of the train window to see Baba still waiting his turn to fill the *surai* when the train began moving. In no time it had reached the end of the platform and left the station; we all panicked. But Baba managed to board a coach at the back and appeared in our compartment like a superhero. He chuckled at the commotion we had created about him being left behind.

Mukund Mama, my maternal uncle, travelled from Aurangabad to meet us at Manmaad, which was a transit stop. He would escort us back to our grandparents' house. Dada, my maternal grandfather, was all set to pamper his grandchildren. He'd arrange a ride on a *taanga* (a horse driven carriage) from Aurangabad station to Ajji's house by Deogiri College. As the *taanga* was pulled across the road, we could see huge trees on both sides of the station road. Each tree was marked with a broad, reddish-brown border at the bottom. I loved counting them every year to check if there were more or less. One, two, three, four….gradually these led to my grandparents' house. Even today, when I visit Maharashtra, the sight of the trees with the brown borders connects me instantly to beautiful, gratifying childhood memories I have of holidays with my grandparents at their home. To me, it is the most beautiful place on earth.

Delicious food, including fresh fruits like grapes, mangoes and watermelons, and plenty of fun marked the holidays. There was a mandatory *chaar cha chaha* (mid-afternoon tea) with *Kaalavlele Pohe* (either mixed with *metkut* or *pud* chutney and served with onions) to snack on. The younger generation had dinner served in the backyard with *Panji* (great-grandmother) whom we fondly called *ek daat waali ajji*, because she just had one tooth left in her mouth. She would sit holding a massive *paraat* of food and the children sat in a semi-circle in front of her. Her modus operandi of feeding us was to place a mouthful on our palms. *Metkut-bhaat* was mixed in the huge plate with helpings of *bhaaji*, *lonche* and chutney. Mealtime was also a story time. *Panji* would make soft balls of rice with an occasional serving of the *bhaaji* hidden within and serve each of us in turn. We ate until the story was over and it was only then that I would realise that she had fed me more than I usually ate!

Smita *mavshi* had lived in Ratnagiri for a few years. She would visit us during our stay. Her arrival meant a supply of Kokan *mewa*, a bounty of goodies from the coastal region. I recall tasting kokum fruit for the first time during one visit. The dining room had a huge wall cupboard holding jars filled with pickles and preserves. I loved sneaking into the cupboard to lay my hands on the jar of tart kokum fruits in sugar.

Radhika *mami* is an excellent cook. She amazes me even more because she had started cooking when she was a teenager. She is very popular when it comes to making goodies for kids – even the adults in the family demand her patented *Aamti* or *Jwarichi Bhaakri*. The secret, of course, is her *Kaalaa masala* along with the other ingredients and the right amount of time, love and care she puts into everything she cooks. She pats paper-thin *Bhaakri* that she would tear into quarters and spread *tup* on!

Radhika Mami's Kaala Masala

Condiments and served on the left side of the plate. These comprise of dry or wet chutney and *Koshimbir*. Fruits, berries, flowers and vegetables like tomatoes guavas, banana, raw mango, gooseberries, *Chinch mohor* (tamarind flowers) and *hadgyachi phule* (vegetable of hummingbird flowers) are used in making a variety of chutneys and *Koshimbir*. Tamarind flowers, when dry roasted and mixed with spices and roasted crushed peanuts make a unique dry chutney.

Metkut, Daangar, dry chutney (*pud* or *daanyachi*) *satuche peeth* and *Yessar Pithi* are essential in a traditional Marathwadi pantry. The variety of dry chutneys in the kitchen is an easy way to give the meal an extra dimension and add variation when you are short of side dishes. Even today, chutney-poli makes for a great last-minute dinner for me when I am in a hurry, or when we are on the road and finding food may be slightly tricky.

Ingredients

Coriander seeds 1 cup

Cumin seeds 1 tbs

Fenugreek seeds 1 tsp

Dry red chillies 1/4 cup (or to taste)

Black stone flower about 20g

Dry coconut half

Asafoetida 1 tsp

Oil 1.5 tbs

Method

Heat ½ tbs oil in a pan. Roast each ingredient, apart from coconut and asafoetida, one at a time. Add more oil if needed.

Roast the coconut half directly on the flame until white part turns brown and chop into pieces.

Mix all the ingredients and grind into a fine powder.

If you are using grated dry coconut or desiccated coconut for the masala, dry roast it in a pan until light brown.

Storage: Store in an air-tight container.

Use: I use this masala for *Aamti* and other vegetable sides.

Daangar

When the pantry is short of ingredients or the refrigerator shelves are empty, *Daangar* often referred as *bharad* in our family, is the perfect solution.

It is a great accompaniment eaten with *polya* or a simple *bhaakri*, providing a significant new dimension and adding nutritional value to a simple meal.

Wheat, harbaraa daal, udid daal when mixed and processed in the ratio of 2:1:1/2 in to coarse flour, it makes another nutritious mix called as *Satuche peeth*.

It includes a simple mix of harbaraa daal, udid daal and rice. Lightly spiced with coriander and cumin seeds, the ground mix can be prepared in advance and stored in an airtight container.

Ingredients

For ground mix

Harbaraa daal 1 cup

Udid daal ½ cup

Rice ¼ cup

Coriander seeds 2 tbs

Cumin seeds 1 tbs

To use the ground mix

Onion or radish 1, finely chopped

Daangar 5 tbs

Water ¼ cup

Thick yoghurt 1 cup

For tempering

Oil, 1 tsp

Asafoetida a pinch

Mustard seeds ½ tsp

Red chillies 2, broken into pieces

Curry leaves 4

Turmeric 1 tsp

Salt and sugar to taste

Chopped coriander for garnishing

Method

In a pan, dry roast all the ingredients. When slightly cooled, grind into a coarse powder. When cool, store in an air-tight container.

To use

In a bowl, mix the *Daangar* with water. Temper with oil, mustard seeds, asafoetida, curry leaves and red chillies. Mix in the chopped onion, yoghurt, salt and sugar. Garnish with chopped coriander.

Metkut

Polya, smeared with *tup* and sprinkled with chutney is my go-to food for my young lad at the university too. Metkut is a great spice mix for certain *bhaaji* or for pepping up *usal*. *Pud* chutney and *metkut* are often used for *Kaalavlele Pohe* to add to the nutty flavours and textures of the various ingredients.

You could use *Metkut* on hot rice. It can also be mixed with yoghurt and seasoned, as you would a chutney. A quick afternoon snack could be *Metkut* added to thinly pounded rice, peanuts, chopped onions and coriander.

Ingredients

Harbaraa daal 2 cups

Udid daal 1 cup

Rice 1/2 cup

Wheat 1/4 cup

Mustard seeds 1/4 cup

Cumin seeds 1.5 tbs

Coriander seeds 2 tsp

Black pepper 2 tsp

Dried red chillies 2-3

Method

Dry roast all the ingredients individually and grind together to a fine powder. Sieve if need be.

To this add

Asafoetida 1 tsp

Turmeric powder two tsp

Mix well and store in an airtight container.

Dry chutney

Dry chutney is a quick accompaniment for a meal.

Kadhi Limbaachi Chutney

Ingredients

Curry leaves washed and patted dry 100g

Daalve (roasted gram daal) 2 tbs

Sesame seeds 1 tsp

Dried red chillies 5-6 or to taste

Asafoetida 1 tsp

Tamarind half a lemon size

or Amsul (kokum) 4-5

Jaggery 1 tbs

Salt to taste

Oil 4 tbs

Method

Heat oil in a pan. Fry each of the ingredients except for jaggery and salt separately and set aside. Fry tamarind or amsul last, (until it becomes crumbly) because it tends to darken the oil. Grind the fried ingredients coarsely together with jaggery and salt.

Store in an air-tight container.

. . . .

Jawas (Flaxseed) Chutney

Ingredients

Jawas 1 cup

Cumin seeds 1 tbs

Red chilli powder 2 tsp

Salt to taste

Method

Dry roast jawas and cumin seeds separately. Grind all the ingredients coarsely together and store in an air-tight container.

Kaaral (Niger Seeds) Chutney

Ingredients

Kaaral 1 cup

Cumin seeds 1 tbs

Red chilli powder 2 tsp

Salt to taste

Method

Dry roast *kaaral* and cumin seeds separately. Grind all the ingredients coarsely together and store in an air-tight container.

....

Tilachi (Sesame Seeds) Chutney

Ingredients

Sesame seeds 1 cup

Cumin seeds 1 tbs

Red chilli powder 2 tsp

Salt to taste

Method

Dry roast sesame seeds and cumin seeds separately. Coarse grind the roasted seeds with red chilli powder and salt. Store in an air-tight container.

....

Khobra Lasun Chutney

Ingredients

Khobra ½

Lasun 8 (or add as preferred)

Cumin seeds 1 tbs

Red chilli powder 2 tsp

Salt to taste

Method

Grate the coconut. Dry roast the grated coconut and cumin seeds separately. Coarse grind the roasted ingredients with garlic, red chilli powder and salt.

Store in an air-tight container.

Daanyachi (Peanuts) Chutney

Ingredients

Peanuts 2 cups, roasted

Red chilli powder 4 tsp

Cumin seeds 1 tbs

Salt to taste

Method

Roasting peanuts for this chutney is slightly tricky.

My mother suggested, "Daane ase bhajayche ki danyala ekahi chatka lagla nahi pahije ani chahubajuni bhajle gele pahije... dane solalyawar te lalsar disle pahijet....asha danyanchi chutey mixer war keli ki hamkhas tel sutata....100 percent." This means, peanuts exude natural oils if roasted on low heat in the right manner without darkening them.

Roast the peanuts on low heat. When they are ready, roast the cumin seeds. Pound these ingredients coarsely together, along with red chilli powder and salt in a heavy iron mortar and pestle (*khal batta*). Alternatively, coarse grinding in a food processor will do the trick.

Store in an air-tight container.

Tip: To remove the skins, fold the roasted peanuts into a towel and rub. This will loosen the skins. Transfer the peanuts on to a plate and blow over them – this will blow off the loose skins. Traditionally, a winnowing fan is used to de-skin roasted peanuts.

Pud Chutney

This can be added to yoghurt or eaten dry with chapaati. It is delicious in *Kalavlele Pohe*.

Ingredients

Udid daal 1 cup, dry roasted and ground coarsely

Harbaraa daal 1 cup, dry roasted and ground coarsely

Sesame seeds 1/2 cup, dry roasted and ground

Dry coconut ½ (or desiccated coconut 1/4 cup)

Coriander seeds 1 tbs, dry roasted and ground

Cumin seeds 1tbs, dry roasted and ground

Dry red chillies 1/2 cup

Tamarind (lemon-sized ball)

Jaggery grated 1 tbs

Salt to taste

Curry leaves ¼ cup, dry roasted and crushed

For tempering

Oil 1 tbs

Mustard seeds 1 tsp

Asafoetida a generous pinch

Red chilli powder 1 tsp (optional)

Method

Place coconut half on an open flame and roast till it changes colour. Chop into small pieces and grind. If you are using desiccated coconut, dry roast it.

Heat a pan with 1 tbs oil. Add curry leaves and fry till crisp. Drain on a kitchen towel.

Into the same oil, add dry red chillies and fry. Drain on a kitchen towel.

Dry roast tamarind in a pan and crush finely. Sieve the powder.

Mix all the ingredients after grinding coarsely, including the curry leaves. Add red chilli powder to this chutney in the tempering if required. Prepare the tempering with mustard seeds and asafoetida. Let it cool. Add tempering to the chutney mix. Mix well and adjust salt, jaggery and tamarind powder to taste.

Store this dry *Pud Chutney* in an air-tight jar. It lasts for about a month.

Tips: You could use amsul instead of tamarind. However, amsul makes the chutney blacker, so it is best to add as little as possible.

Thecha

Ingredients

Green chillies 15

Garlic cloves 5-6

Chopped coriander (optional)

Methi seeds ¼ tsp

Asafoetida a pinch

Mustard seeds ½ tsp

Turmeric ½ tsp

Salt to taste

Sugar Oil 2 tbs

Method

Temper hot oil with mustard, methi seeds, asafoetida and turmeric. Add the chillies and garlic. Saute these in oil until the green chillies and garlic are slightly cooked but still have a bite. Turn the heat off. Add salt, sugar and fresh coriander. Using a rawi(a wooden buttermilk churner) crush the mix roughly. Squeeze lemon juice for tang.

Thecha acquires a smoky taste if the green chillies and the garlic are cooked directly on fire. This smoky version makes a delicious dip when mixed with yoghurt.

Options

Red chillies can be used to make *ranjakaa*.

When coarsely ground raw peanuts are added to *thecha* it becomes another condiment, colloquially referred to as *khardaa*. Thecha, ranjakaa or khardaa are perfect to pair with any flatbread or rice preparation.

Pohyacha Bhurka

Ingredients

Pounded rice ¼ cup

Daalve (roasted gram daal) 1 tbs

Peanuts 1 tbs

Asafoetida 1/8 tsp

Red chilli powder 1 tsp

Salt to taste

Oil 4 tbs

Mustard seeds 1 tsp

Method

Place a pan on low heat; add three tablespoons of oil, add all the ingredients except mustard seeds, asafoetida, salt and red chilli powder. Stir till nicely fried. Turn the heat off and add red chilli powder and salt. Cool and grind coarsely. In a *kadla* (a deep vessel used for tempering), heat oil, temper mustard seeds asafoetida, salt and red chilli powder.

Bhurka can be served along with *ukad shengule*, ukad, khichadi or along with our daily meals.

Lasunachaa Bhurka

Aai makes this quite often to go along with *Khichadi* and *Saar*. I like using sesame seeds in this *Bhurka*. My cousin Shruti Degloorkar suggests using ground peanuts.

Ingredients

Garlic cloves 10-15, chopped

Red chilli powder 2 tsp (or to taste)

Sesame seeds or coarsely ground Peanuts 2 tbs

Salt to taste

Oil 2 tbs

Mustard seeds 1 tsp

Asafoetida a pinch

Method

Heat oil in a *kadhai*. Temper with mustard seeds and asafoetida. Add chopped garlic and cook for a couple of minutes. Add sesame seeds or coarsely ground peanuts and stir on low heat until the garlic cooks and turns crisp. Turn the heat off and add chilli powder and salt. Mix well and serve with piping hot *Khichadi* or *Polya* or drizzle over *Ukad Pendi*.

Methamba

Ingredients

Raw mangoes 2

Fenugreek seeds 1 tsp

Jaggery 2 tbs, grated

Red chilli powder 1 tsp

Mustard seeds 1 tsp

Asafoetida a pinch

Turmeric 1 tsp

Oil 2 tbs

Method

Cook the mangoes and extract the flesh. In a teaspoon of oil, roast fenugreek seeds till light pink. Grind to a fine powder. In a pan heat oil and temper with mustard seeds and asafoetida. Add turmeric and red chilli powder, then the mashed mango flesh and jaggery. Mix well and simmer for a few minutes. Stir continuously and bring to a boil before turning off the heat. Cool and serve.

Note: Instead of cooking the mangoes, one can chop them and cook in a vessel.

Smita Mavshi's *Sakhubadda* too is made using the same spices but the method differs slightly. Instead of cooking the mango, it is chopped finely and mixed with the spices including mustard powder, red chilli powder, roasted and ground fenugreek seeds, salt, roasted sesame powder, asafoetida and jaggery. This is set aside for a couple of days in a vessel to allow the spices to flavour the mixture; the mango pieces soften in the juices it exudes while it is on the side. When topped with a *khamang* phodni, it makes a delicious accompaniment to serve with the meals.

Takku can be made when raw mango and raw onions are mixed with the tempering and spices mentioned above for *methamba*.

Kaairas/Panchaamrut

Ingredients

Bitter gourd/Kaarla 1,
chopped in roundels

Oil 2 tbs

Mustard seeds 1 tsp

Kaala masala 2 tsp

Asafoetida a pinch

Curry leaves a few

Turmeric 1 tsp

Green chillies 4, chopped

Sesame seeds 2 tbs, roasted
and ground

Roasted peanuts 2 tbs

Jaggery 1 tbs

Tamarind pulp one tsp

Salt to taste

Warm water 1 cup

Coriander for garnishing

Method

Place a pan on medium heat. Temper oil with mustard seeds, asafoetida, turmeric and curry leaves. Add chopped green chillies and peanuts. Add bitter gourd. Mix tamarind pulp, jaggery, Kaala masala and salt. Add ground sesame seeds. Add warm water and bring to a boil. Kaairas is often made on special occasions when the family eats a traditional meal. I love it with the sweet *Puran Poli*!

Naaralaachi Chutney

Ingredients

Shredded fresh coconut
1 cup

Green chillies 2-3

Cumin seeds roasted 2 tsp

Salt to taste

Sugar 1/4 tsp

Lemon juice 1 tbs

For the tempering

Oil 2 tsp

Mustard seeds 1 tsp

Asafoetida 1 pinch

Curry leaves 5-6

Method

Blend together shredded coconut, green chillies, cumin seeds, salt, sugar and lemon juice to a smooth paste. Use 1 tablespoon of water to grind it smoothly if needed. Add coriander to enhance the taste if you like. Temper oil with mustard seeds, asafoetida and curry leaves and pour over the chutney.

· ·

Hirvya Tomatochi Chutney

Ingredients

Green tomatoes 4, chopped

Green chillies 2, chopped

Coriander ¼ cup

Sesame seeds or crushed
peanuts 2 tbs

Jaggery 1 tbs

Salt to taste

Mustard seeds one tsp

Asafoetida a pinch

Turmeric 1 tsp

Oil 2 tbss

Method

In a pan heat oil and temper with mustard seeds and asafoetida. Add turmeric, green chillies and sesame seeds (if using) and saute for a minute. Add chopped green tomatoes. Stir and cover to cook until the tomatoes soften slightly. Add chopped coriander, jaggery and salt. Mix well and cook till the jaggery melts. Add the crushed peanuts. Turn the heat off and let it cool. Once cool, grind into a coarse chutney.

Aalyaachi Chutney

Ingredients

Ginger 25gm

Salt to taste

Sugar ¼ tsp

Lemon juice ¼ cup

Cumin seeds one tsp

Asafoetida a pinch

Oil 1 tbs

Method

Either use a *paata varvantaa* or a grinder to make this chutney. Place the ingredients in a bowl and squeeze lemon juice over – the colour will change to a lovely red. Just before you serve, temper with cumin and asafoetida in oil. *Aalyaachi Chutney* is an excellent palate cleanser.

· ·

Dodkyaanchya Sheeranchi Chutney

Ingredients

Dodke sheer (peels) using 4-5 ridge gourds

Sesame seeds 1 tsp

Red chilli powder 1 tsp

Salt to taste

Mustard seeds 1 tsp

Asafoetida a pinch

Turmeric ½ tsp

Oil 2 tbs

Method

In a pan heat oil and temper with mustard seeds and asafoetida. Add turmeric, red chilli powder and sesame seeds. Add the dodke peels and stir until crisp. Add salt and grind coarsely to make the most delicious chutney which has an interesting nomenclature in our family as *raaja-raani*.

Amsulaachi Chutney

Ingredients

Amsul 8, soaked in warm
water for half an hour

Jaggery 2 tbs, grated

Red chilli powder 1 tsp

Roasted cumin powder 1 tsp

Salt to taste

Method

Blend all the ingredients to make a smooth paste. Decant into
a bowl and serve.

. . . .

Gaajarachi Koshimbir

Ingredients

Carrots 2, grated

Moog daal 2 tbs, soaked for
half an hour

Lemon juice 2 tsp

Salt to taste

Sugar ¼ tsp

Mustard seeds 1 tsp

Asafoetida a pinch

Turmeric ½ tsp

Oil 2 tbs

Curry leaves 4

Green chilli 1, chopped

Method

In a bowl gently mix grated carrots and moog daal. Add lemon
juice and season with salt and sugar. In a pan heat oil and
temper with mustard seeds, asafoetida and turmeric. Add curry
leaves and green chilli. Sauté for a couple of minutes. Add this
tempering to the *koshimbir*.

A *Paapad* or a *Saandge Mirchi* fried and crushed on to this
koshimbir adds a lovely crunch.

Another way to make this *koshimbir* is to add yoghurt to the
grated carrots. Avoid using moog daal and lemon juice, but
follow the rest of the recipe.

Kaakdichi Koshimbir

Ingredients

Kaakdi 1, finely chopped (*chochun*)

Peanuts 1 tbs, roasted and crushed

Lemon juice 2 tsp

Salt to taste

Sugar ¼ tsp

Mustard seeds 1 tsp

Asafoetida a pinch

Turmeric ½ tsp

Oil 2 tbs

Curry leaves 4

Green chilli 1, chopped

Method

In a bowl mix cucumber and crushed peanuts. Add lemon juice; season with salt and sugar. Temper hot oil with mustard seeds, asafoetida and turmeric. Add curry leaves and green chilli. Sauté for a few minutes. Add this tempering to the *koshimbir* or *khamang kaakdi*.

You can use yoghurt instead of lemon juice to make a another cooling koshimbir.

. . . .

Khudlelya Methichi Koshimbir

Methi leaves release more flavour and aroma if bruised through tearing rather than being cut. Thus this *koshimbir* is made using torn methi leaves.

Ingredients

Methi 1 bunch, sorted and torn to get two cups of leaves

Turmeric 1 tsp

Red chilli powder 1 tsp

Peanuts 1 tbs, roasted and crushed coarsely

Oil 2 tsp

Mustard seeds 1 tsp

Asafoetida, 1 pinch

Salt and sugar to taste

Juice of half a lemon

Method

To the torn leaves, add a generous sprinkling of crushed peanuts. Temper with mustard seeds and asafoetida; followed by turmeric and red chilli powder. Add sugar and season with salt. Add lemon juice and mix well.

Snacks and Quick Bites

Vijaya Itoikar, Saroja Kulkarni, Sudha Pade and Pratibha Kulkarni

Warmth of Old Cotton

I recall summer afternoons spent at Ambejogai Wada. While us kids played *gola phuli* (tic-tac-toe) drawn on the floor with *khadu* (chalk) or set up our kitchen for role play on the stone steps, Tai would sit on the *satranji* layering her old *lugada* or saree. Each *lugada* was folded into layers and cut into geometric patterns that would be hand-stitched to make *godhadi*, a quilt.

Tai would collect fabrics lying around the house, especially those that needed new life. A simple running stitch held the layers together. There was no rule for the shape, size or type of fabric, but when put together, it created a beautiful pattern.

The same ritual was followed every afternoon when Tai stitched the layered fabrics together with white thread. Each *godhadi* took shape as a beautiful and warm blanket in a few days. Every day, someone would join in and help align the pieces. It was a way for the women in the house to come together and chat, sometimes in whispers. It was the time when they could share their grumbles, have a good laugh, gossip or just speak of things concerning the family, each other and women in general. Tai would listen to it all; she knew that being a good listener was a remarkable job. She suggested tips to the girls and gave advice on the ways of life, nodding now and then as she continued with her work.

As a child I recall sitting on the unfinished *godhadi* to keep the layers in place while Tai's nimble fingers ran the needle through the fabric to put it all together. It was handling by her experienced hands that made the fabric softer, and the *godhadi* had a good life.

By the time she finished layering and stitching together the fabric scraps, it was time for the menfolk to be given afternoon tea. Tai would hastily roll up her work and chivvy the other women to help her in the kitchen to make mid-afternoon snacks for the children and tea for the rest of the family. It was a tricky task getting the *chul* lit. It meant someone had to make sure the wood chips were dry and fetch a stock of *gaurya* (cow dung patties). Tai would sprinkle kerosene on the wood to start the fire. Once the tea had reached everyone in the *diwan ghar* and to Grandfather in his room, the women gathered around the *chul* to sip their share. Then began the chores to cook the evening meal. *Char cha chaha* was always accompanied by snacks made for the youngsters in the family. A quick-fix snack made with shredded left over polya like tukde often called as *phodnichi poli* or even *dudh-poli* and at times *policha laadu* would calm down our *choti bhook* (small hunger pangs).

Ukadpendi

Ukadpendi is steamed snack made with whole wheat flour or gluten-free and high-protein sorghum flour. A thinner version of this *Ukadpendi* makes a wholesome soup!

Ingredients

Roasted wheat flour or jowar flour 3 cups

Crushed peanuts 1 tbs

Onion 1, chopped

Garlic cloves 2-3

Green chillies 2

Curry leaves 4-5

Oil 2 tbs

Mustard seeds 1 tsp

Turmeric 1 tsp

Asafoetida a pinch

Salt to taste

Jaggery 1 tsp

Tamarind pulp 2 tsp

Water 1.5 cups

Method

In a pan, temper oil with mustard seeds, asafoetida and turmeric. Add garlic, green chillies and onions. Saute well. Add water. When water begins to boil, add the roasted flour and stir to avoid lumps. Cover and cook for 5 minutes. Garnish with chopped coriander and serve hot.

Option: *Mokali bhaajni* can be made in a similar way using *thaalipith bhaajni*.

Upma

Ingredients

Fine semolina 1 cup

Cumin seeds 1 tsp

Asafoetida 1 pinch

Curry leaves 5-6

Green chillies 2, finely chopped

Peanuts ¼ cup

Udid daal 1 tsp

Onion 1, finely chopped

Ginger grated 1/2 tsp

Salt to taste

Oil or tup 2 tbs

Sugar ½ tsp

Water 1.5 cups

Chopped coriander and fresh grated coconut for garnishing

Method

Roast semolina in a pan until light pink and it wafts of a beautiful aroma. Set aside in a plate.

In the same pan, pour oil or *tup* if using; temper with cumin seeds, Udid daal, curry leaves, asafoetida and sauté for half a minute. To this add green chillies, peanuts and cook until the peanuts are not raw. Sauté onions until translucent. Pour water into the pan; season with salt and sugar. Once the water begins to boil, turn the heat to low.

Add roasted semolina gradually, a spoon at a time and stirring continuously to avoid forming lumps of semolina. Cover and let steam at a low temperature for 4-5 minutes.

Serve piping hot upma in plates or bowls; garnish with chopped coriander and fresh shredded coconut and a piece of lemon.

Tip: Yermalkar ajji uses tomatoes as well in her upma which is added after cooking onions.

Pohe

Ingredients

Medium pounded rice 2 cups washed and drained (these soften when washed in water)

Onion chopped finely 1

Peanuts ¼ cup

Green chillies chopped 2

Oil 3 tbss

Mustard seeds 1 tsp

Turmeric 1 tsp

Curry leaves a sprig

Salt to taste

Sugar ½ tsp

Lemon juice 1 tsp

Chopped coriander to garnish

Method

Heat oil in a pan. Temper with mustard seeds, curry leaves and green chillies; add peanuts and sauté. Once the peanuts are done, add turmeric and empty the softened pounded rice. Season with salt and sugar and mix well. Cover and steam on a low heat for 3-4 minutes. Uncover, add lemon juice and mix well. Cover and steam for another 3-4 minutes.

Garnish with chopped coriander and a wedge of lemon.

Sushila

A snack similar to *Pohe* is a quick fix for unexplained holiday hunger pangs! If one is making *tukde* or *phodnichi poli*, you follow the same recipe replacing puffed rice with 2 bowls of shredded polya.

Ingredients

Churmure (puffed rice) 4 cups, soaked in water

Onion 1, chopped finely

Peanuts 1/4 cup

Green chillies 2, chopped

Coriander for garnishing

Half a lemon

Sugar 1/4 tsp (optional)

For the tempering

Mustard seeds one tsp

Curry leaves 5-6

Turmeric 1/2 tsp

Oil 1 tbs

Method

Drain and squeeze the water from the puffed rice. Set aside.

Set a pan on medium heat. Add oil and temper with mustard seeds. Add chopped green chillies, curry leaves and peanuts. Stir for a minute. Add the onions and turmeric. Stir till the onions are translucent.

Add the puffed rice and salt and mix well. Add 1/4 tsp sugar if you like. Cover and steam briefly.

Turn the heat off. Squeeze in lemon juice. Mix well.

Garnish with chopped coriander and serve.

Dadpe Pohe

Ingredients

Paatal pohe(thin pounded rice) 2 cups dry roasted and set aside

Onions finely chopped 2

Coriander chopped ¼ cup

Green chillies finely chopped 3-4

Curry leaves 2 springs

Fresh coconut grated 1 cup

Roasted peanuts ¼ cup

Oil 2 tbs

Mustard seeds 1 tsp

Turmeric 1 tsp

Asafoetida 1 pinch

Salt to taste

Sugar 1 tsp

Lemon juice from quarter lemon

Metkut 1 tbs (optional)

Method

In a bowl mix *paatal pohe* and shredded coconut, cover and set aside for 20 minutes under a weight.

In a *kadhla* (small pan for tempering) heat oil and temper with mustard seeds, asafoetida, curry leaves and add turmeric.

Add the tempering, metkut, salt, sugar, green chillies, chopped onions, lemon juice and chopped coriander to the pohe-coconut mix and mix well.

Serve immediately. A tangy tip to make this version of *dadpe pohe –dadaplele* (compressed with weight) – my sister Shruti's family relishes dadpe pohe with grated raw mango during summer.

Kaalavlele Pohe

Ingredients

Paatal pohe(thin pounded rice) 2 cups dry roasted and set aside

Curry leaves 2 springs

Dry coconut grated and roasted 1 cup

Roasted peanuts ¼ cup

Daalve ¼ cup

Oil 2 tbs

Mustard seeds 1 tsp

Turmeric 1 tsp

Red chilli powder 1 tsp

Asafoetida 1 pinch

Salt to taste

Sugar 1 tsp

Metkut 1 tbs

Pud chutney 2 tbss

Method

In a *kadhla* (small pan for tempering) heat oil and temper with mustard seeds, asafoetida, curry leaves; add turmeric and red chilli powder. Add peanuts and *daalva* to roast in oil. Turn the heat off.

Take roasted pohe in a bowl; add the tempering, *metkut, pud chutney*, salt, sugar, grated coconut and mix well.

Optional:

Onion finely chopped 1

Coriander chopped ¼ cup

One may use the onions and coriander to serve on these pohe.

Chivda

Ingredients

Thin Pohe roasted 2 kg

Oil for tempering and frying the ingredients 1 cup

Curry leaves few sprigs

Peanuts 1 cup

Cashews 1 cup

Red chillies 2-3

Tempering

Mustard seeds 2 tsp

Turmeric powder 2 tsp

Carom seeds 1 tsp

asafoetida 1/2 tsp

Cumin powder 1.5 tbsp

Coriander powder 3 tbsp

Oil for tempering

Salt to taste

Sugar 1 tsp

Method

Fry the peanuts, curry leaves, cashews, red chillies separately and drain on tissue paper. Traditionally pohe are tied in a cloth and sun dried or dry roasted in kadhai. I roast them in oven. Instead of oven, one may carry out the process in a kadhai for the rest of the recipe.

Preheat the oven to 160 degrees C. In two roasting pans, spread the thin pohe and roast till crisp. This will take about 20-25 mins. Once the pohe are roasted, add in the fried ingredients apart from the tempering ingredients.

Tempering

Heat oil just under the smoking point. Add in the mustard seeds till they splutter. Add the asafoetida and carom seeds. Add cumin and coriander powder. Turn the heat off and add salt and sugar.

Mixing

Add the tempering to the roasted pohe and the fried ingredients. Mix well till everything is coated with the tempering and the masala.

Place the well coated pohe in the oven again and roast for 10 mins at the same temperature.

Cool and store in air tight container. This proves to be a good snack with tea.

Lonche Pohe

Ingredients

Paatal pohe(thin pounded rice) 2 cups dry roasted and set aside

Onions finely chopped 2

Coriander chopped ¼ cup

Kairee lonchyache khaar(masala from raw mango pickle) 2 tbss

Oil 2 tbs

Salt only if required

Sugar 1 tsp

Method

Place pohe in a bowl; to this add oil, lonche khaar, sugar and mix well till the khaar coats pohe well enough. Mix chopped onions and chopped coriander and mix well. Lonche khaar has enough salt so one may not additional salt.

. . . .

Chakli

To make bhaajani

Ingredients

Rice 2 cups

Harbaraa daal 1 cup

Udid daal ½ cup

Moog daal ½ cup

Sabudana ¼ cup

Coriander seeds 2 cup

Cumin seeds ¼ cup

Method

The traditional method of making *chakli* bhaajni can sound tedious however it tends to help make the crunchiest of chakli one can ever have. All the ingredients apart from the spices and sabudana need washing individually and drying in shade. Once dry, each of the ingredients including sabudana and the spices are roasted on a low heat. Once roasted, let cool and grind into fine flour.

To make chakli

Ingredients

Chakli bhaajni 1 cup

Turmeric ½ tsp

Red chilli powder ½ tsp

Sesame seeds ½ tsp

Carom seeds ½ tsp

Asafoetida a pinch

Salt to taste

Oil heated(mohan) 2 tbs

Water ½ cup

Method

Mix all the ingredients to make a soft, pliable dough. Prepare a *chakli* press (*sorya* in Marathi). Fill the sorya with a piece of dough and begin pressing into concentric round or spirals. Refill with more dough when the first portion is used up. If you prefer pressing *chakli* in advance, cover to avoid chakli getting dry. Alternatively, you can begin frying immediately.

Heat oil. Gently slide a couple of *chakli* into the hot oil. With a slotted spoon, splash hot oil from the *kadhai* over each *chakli*. Flip in the oil and fry until golden brown.

Drain on a paper towel and continue making the rest of the *chakli*.

Frying continuously can bring down the temperature of the oil. To make sure it is at the right temperature, take a break and heat it once again to the desired temperature.

Note: When the dough is rolled into a thin, long sausage with hands and made into either a loop or spiral, the same snack is called as Kadbole.

Quick Chakli

My mother-in-law suggested using boiled *moog daal* with steamed *maida* or *kanik* for instant *chakli*. She suggested tying flour in muslin and steaming in a pressure cooker with the *daal*. Instead of whole wheat you could use gram flour or jowar flour.

Ingredients

Plain flour 4 cups

Moog dal ½ cup

Turmeric 1 tsp

Red chilli powder 1 tsp

Asafoetida a generous pinch

Coriander powder 1 tsp

Sesame seeds 1 tsp

Carom seeds 1 tsp

Salt to taste

Oil for frying

Method

Wash ½ cup moog dal and pressure cook in 1.5 cups of water.

Steam 4 cups plain flour in a pressure cooker without the whistle for 20 minutes (Tie the flour in muslin and place it in a vessel). Once steamed, sieve the flour.

Make a paste of the flour with approximately 1 cup of water.

Add turmeric, red chilli powder, asafoetida, coriander powder, sesame seeds, carom seeds and salt to the steamed and sieved flour.

Using the *moog daal* paste, make a smooth dough with the prepared flour. Cover and set aside.

Heat the oil in a pan that needs to be deep enough to hold the oil and 6-8 *chakli* .

Using the *sorya* pipe the spirals.

When the oil is hot, drop in the *chakli* and fry on medium heat till golden brown. Drain on a paper towel and store in an air-tight container.

Varan-Battya

Varan-battya is a version of the traditional Rajasthani preparation *Daal-Baati*. Jalna, our town in Maharashtra has been influenced by Rajasthani culture, due to the tradesmen from that state residing there. Hence a few of their rituals and foods were soon amalgamated into the local culture. *Daal-baati* is conventionally prepared in a pit dug in the ground and roasted on burning embers. My mother-in-law prepared the *Battya* (in Marathi) in a gas oven.

Battya are served with *Thecha* made with green chillies and *Ambat Varan*.

For the **Battyas**

Ingredients	Method
Clarified butter 2 cups, melted	Mix all the ingredients except clarified butter and make a soft dough with water. Cover with a wet cloth and set aside for 15 mins.
Semolina 2 cups	
Whole wheat flour 4 cups	Make small balls of dough. In each ball, make a well. Into this well, squeeze in a small piece of dough that has been soaked in clarified butter.
Vegetable oil 3 tbs	

Roll the dough ball into a slightly flattened disc.

Use the rest of the dough to prepare these discs.

Drop each ball into boiling water for a couple of minutes, then remove, drain and put into the oven. Bake the balls on high heat (180°C) for 20 mins on one side till golden brown and then turn each one over. Make sure that these are baked completely – the dough inside needs to be fully cooked as well. These balls can also be deep fried.

Crush the baked balls slightly (retaining the shape) and soak them in the clarified butter for at least an hour. Serve with piping hot *Ambat Varan*. Crush the *Battyas* into the daal and relish!

Misal Paav

Misal Paav is a one of best-loved street food which now is our family favourite too. For the Misal, I use Mami's kaalaa masala. To this I add fresh masala made by roasting onion on the flame and sautéing garlic and dry coconut in oil. Alternatively, roast 1/2 onion and 2 garlic cloves sautéed with a 2 tsp of oil (till brown). Cool. Add 2 tbs of Mami's masala to the sautéed onion and garlic.

Ingredients

For making sprouts

Sprouted Moth beans 1 cup

Oil 1 tbs

Cumin seeds ½ tsp

Asafoetida a pinch

Turmeric ½ tsp

Chilli powder ½ tsp

Kaalaa masala 1 tbs

Tamarind pulp 1 tsp

Jaggery 1 tsp

Salt to taste

For making Kat/Tarri

Oil 1 tsp

Asafoetida a pinch

Cumin seeds ½ tsp

Turmeric ½ tsp

Red chilli pd 2 tbs

Jaggery 1 tsp

Tamarind pulp 2 tsp

Salt to taste

Kaalaa masala (used in Marathi preparations)

For assembling

Boiled potatoes 2, chopped

Tomatoes 1 cup, chopped

Onion 1 cup, chopped

Coriander ½ cup, chopped

Lemon quarters

Farsaan/ Shev to taste

Method

Temper oil with asafoetida and cumin seeds. Add the sprouts and the rest of the ingredients for the sprouts. Mix. Add 1.5 cups of water and pressure cook two whistles.

To make the Kat/Tarri

Temper 1 tsp oil with cumin seeds. Add asafoetida. In a bowl, mix turmeric, Kaalaa masala, red chilli powder, salt, jaggery and tamarind pulp. Add to the tempering and stir. Add 2 cups of water and simmer. Place this kat in a different bowl.

When assembling Misal

Into a bowl, spoon two tbs cooked sprouts. Add 1tbs *Farsaan*. Top with a little boiled potato, chopped onions and tomatoes. Add a ladleful of *kat*. Garnish with coriander. Serve with pav (buns) or bread.

. . . .

Bataatyaache Vade

Ingredients

Potatoes 4, boiled, peeled and mashed

Curry leaves 5-6

Green chillies 2

Ginger an inch cube

Garlic cloves 3

Oil 2 tbs

Mustard seeds 1 tsp

Asafoetida 1 pinch

Turmeric 1 tsp

Lemon juice 3 tbs

Coriander ¼ cup, chopped

Sugar ½ tsp

Salt to taste

Grind ginger, garlic and green chillies to a paste.

For the batter

Gram flour ¾ cup

Turmeric ½ tsp

Water ½ cup

Salt ½ tsp

Oil for deep frying

Method

Temper oil with mustard seeds, curry leaves and asafoetida, followed by turmeric. Add green chillies-garlic-ginger paste and saute for a couple of minutes. Add potatoes, salt and sugar. Mix well so that the oil flavoured with the spices and turmeric coats the mashed potato. Cook for two minutes. Add lemon juice and chopped coriander. Mix well and make equal sized balls and set aside.

In a bowl mix gram flour, turmeric and salt. Add water gradually to make a batter of a consistency to coat the potato balls.

Heat oil in a deep pan. Turn the heat to medium. Dip rolled potato balls in the gram flour batter until each is well-coated. drop gently into the hot oil and fry to a golden brown colour. Drain on paper towels.

Serve with green chutney and fried green chillies sprinkled with salt.

Fritters

Bhaji or fritters are an essential part of the main meal and also makes a great snack, especially on a rainy day. *Kanda (onion) Bhaji* tops the list of favourite fried food. Other vegetables like spinach, Indian borage (owyache paan), potato, capsicum, chillies stuffed with boiled-spiced potatoes, and aubergine also make the most exciting *bhaji*. Vegetables mentioned are sliced thinly into roundels where as with green leafy vegetables single leaves are dipped in the batter and deep fried.

Ingredients

Gram flour ¾ cup

Turmeric ½ tsp

Water ½ cup

Salt ½ tsp

Oil for deep frying

Vegetable of your choice

Method

In a bowl mix gram flour, turmeric and salt. Add water gradually to make a batter of a consistency that can coat the vegetable.

Heat oil in a deep pan. Turn the heat to medium. Dip a couple of pieces of vegetable in the batter until each is well-coated. drop gently into the hot oil and fry to a golden brown colour. Drain on a paper towel.

Serve with green chutney.

Note: Adding 1/2 tsp of carom seeds to the batter enhances the fritter taste.

Kaanda Bhaji

Ingredients

Onions 2, sliced thin

Gram flour about 3 tbs

Carom seeds ½ tsp

Turmeric ½ tsp

Red chilli powder 1 tsp

Asafoetida 1 pinch

Salt to taste

Oil for frying

Method

Mix all the ingredients apart from gram flour. Cover and set aside for 10 mins. Mix in gram flour to coat the chopped onions. The onions marinated with the salt and spices exudes enough water for the gram flour to coat them. Heat oil in a pan. Fry the onion bhaji till brown and crisp. Drain on paper towels. Relish with a hot cup of tea! These bhaji are often called as khekda bhaji.

Note: Sprinkle with cumin powder for the added flavour after frying the kaanda bhaji.

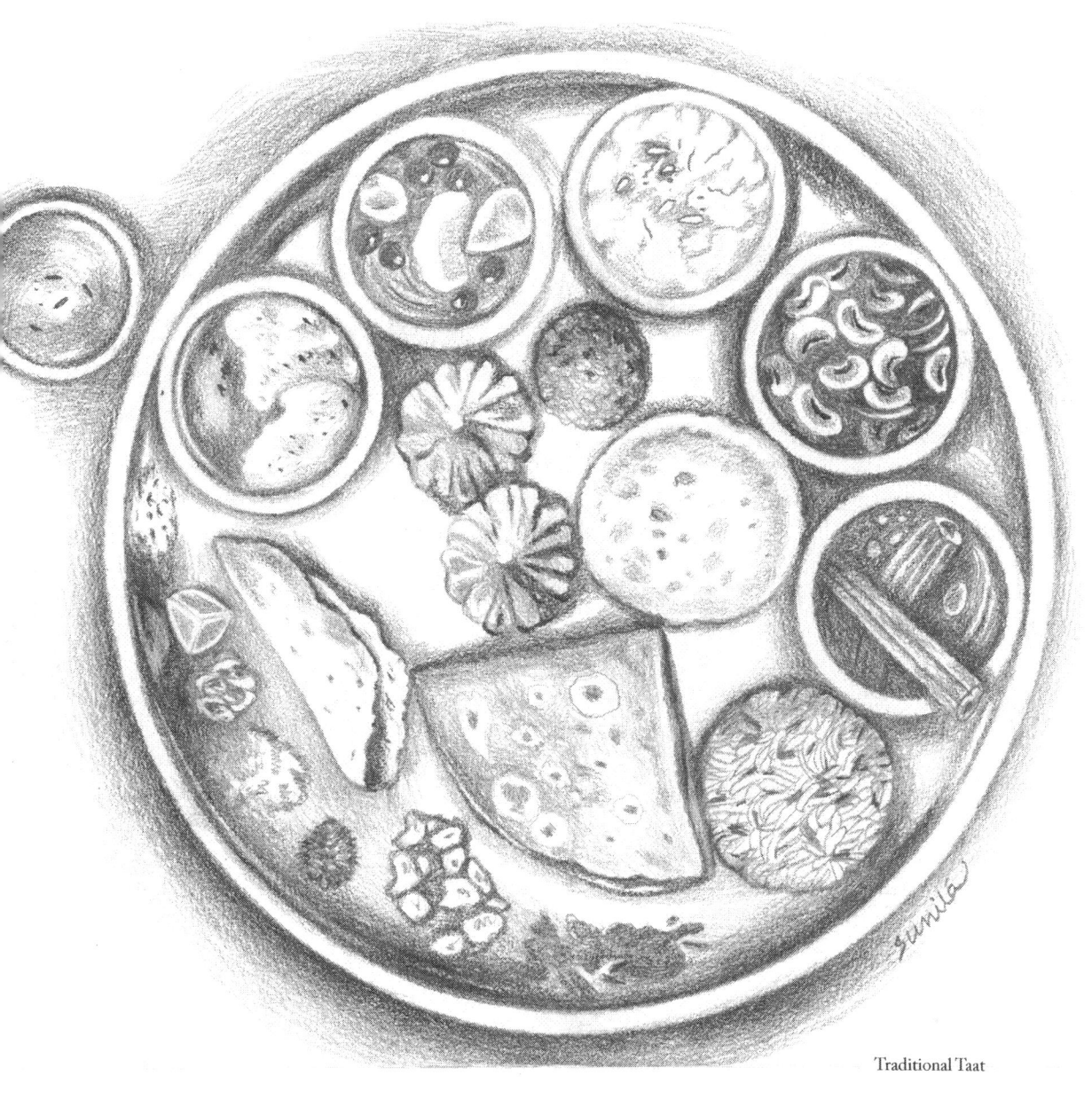

Traditional Taat

Rice Preparations

Paat Paani

Traditionally meals in a Maharashtrian household are served on a banana leaf or a large *thaali* (metal plate). A fabric *aasan* (seat) or a short-legged wooden stool called *paat* is placed to sit on while the meal is being served. For a special occasion, the plate is placed on a *chaurang*, a slightly taller, square wooden stool. When there is a large gathering for a festive occasion or a wedding, *pangat* – an organised seating arrangement – seats guests in rows to allow quick and easy serving of food. The host and the diners put their hands together to chant the traditional food prayer written by Samarth Ramdaas Swami. The atmosphere resonates with *Vadani Kaval Ghetaa Naam Ghyaa Shri Hariche*. Conveying an acknowlegement to *Poornabrahma*, the Supreme. Thus by showing humility and gratification to God, food transmits energy into our lives.

Just before they begin the meal, men set morsels of food aside on the plate and sprinkle water around their dishes, chanting a sacred stotra, thus paying obeisance to the deities and thanking them for the food served. Such practices were traditionally observed because the houses had mud floors. Once dry and loose, there were possibilities of dust contamination in food. Sprinkling water settled the dust and stopped ants or other insects crawling into the plates. Today our houses are modernised but this ritual still continues to offer the first morsel acknowledging gratitude to Goddess Earth. This ritual is also a common practice when *Naivedya* or sweets are offered to deities on festive occasions.

Meals served on a banana leaf or a *taat* make for an unambiguous way of serving food. Multicourse Marathi cuisine is plated with salt, lemon and the condiments including pickles, chutney – both wet and dry – and koshimbir on the left side of the plate; the sides like *phal bhaaji* and *paatal bhaaji, aamti* and *kadhi* are served on the right. Rice, breads and the fried accompaniments take centre stage along with desserts. Foods served on the left side are piquant and eaten with the main meal to add flavour; these are served in very small portions. The individual sides on the right provide the required vitamins, minerals, dietary fibres and proteins, and are savoured in larger quantities. The carbohydrates and starch occupy the main area on the plate. A small portion of rice and *saadha varan* with *tup* is devoured first, before the rest of the meal. Once the meal is over, a humble gratitude is conveyed to the farmers and the people who have cooked the meal with the words *Anna Daata Sukhi Bhawa.*

During my visits to Jalna, I have had beautiful experiences bonding with nature. One fascinating Marathi custom I experienced was *Gograas*, or feeding the cows every day. Herds of cattle went past our house during the late afternoons. At times a couple of cows would stray and stand by our gate to chew on the leaves of the jambul tree and rest in the shade of the branches. My mother-in-law would usher us to the gate to offer *gograas* or a *tukda*, a piece of *poli* or *bhaakri* or some leftover rice to these animals. No food was wasted in the house. With this subtle act of giving, compassion for another living being, donating and sacrificing for animal welfare are exemplified.

The following section explores rice and the variations we have in our family.

Similar phrasing to be used for each category Rice provides starch in meals and is responsible for balancing the amino acid profile required by the body when served in combination with *Daal, Aamti* or yogurt. No meal is considered complete without a serving of rice.

Saadhaa Bhaat

Rice was often cooked in a normal vessel by our grandmothers however, pressure cooker is often used to make steamed rice these days. *Saadhaa Bhaat* is served in the main meal with *Saadha Varan* at the beginning and with *Aamti* later.

Ingredients

Rice 1 cup

Water 1.5 cup (for small grain rice. Long grain rice requires twice the volume of water)

Method

Wash the rice, changing the water until it runs clear.

Place rice and water in a pan that will fit into the pressure cooker. Turn the heat to medium. Once the steam begins to build up, allow the rice to cook for 3 whistles and then turn the heat to low for 5 minutes. Turn off the heat and let the steam escape. Take out the cooked rice and serve with *Saadha Varan* or A*amti*.

Rice with *Metkut*, salt and clarified butter is my comfort food.

Gulgulit mau bhaat, mushy rice is good convalescent food. It is made by cooking rice with more water in the ratio 1:3. *Metkut*, clarified butter, salt and a dash of lime or even a fried *Paapad* and lime pickle with this gruel-like *gulgulit* rice is a great way to counter lack of appetite.

Phodnicha Bhaat

Ingredients

Cooked rice 1 cup

Oil 1 tbs

Mustard 1 tsp

Asafoetida a pinch

Turmeric 1 tsp

Peanuts ¼ cup

Curry leaves 4-5

Green chillies 2, chopped

Onion finely 1, chopped

Salt to taste

Chopped coriander for garnishing

Method

Fluff up the rice with a fork.

Heat oil in a pan. Temper with mustard seeds, asafoetida and curry leaves. Add green chillies and sauté for a minute. Add turmeric and peanuts, followed by chopped onions; fry until the raw taste is gone. Turn the heat off. Pour this tempering over the rice. Add salt and mix well. Garnish with coriander.

Phodnicha Bhaat is a great way of using up leftover rice. I prefer eating it with yogurt or pickle.

Chitranna

Ingredients

Cooked rice 2 cups

Oil 2 tbs

Harbaraa daal 1 tbs, soaked

Raw mango 1 cup, grated

Mustard 1 tsp

Asafoetida a pinch

Turmeric 1 tsp

Peanuts ¼ cup

Dried red chillies 2

Salt to taste

Sugar 1 tsp

Chopped coriander for garnishing

Method

Fluff up the rice with a fork.

Heat oil in a pan. Temper with mustard seeds, asafoetida and curry leaves. Add dry red chillies and sauté for a minute. Add turmeric, Harbaraa daal and peanuts, and fry until the raw taste is gone. Pour this tempering over the rice. Add grated mango and salt and mix well. Garnish with coriander.

Instead of grated mango, you may use lemon juice. Adding *Metkut* to this dish gives it a nutty flavour.

Masaale Bhaat

Masaale Bhaat is synonymous with Marathi weddings or special occasions. It is made with potatoes, cauliflower, peas or ivy gourd.

Ingredients

Rice 2 cups

Ivy gourd 1 cup quartered

kaalaa masala 2 tsp

Jaggery 1 tsp

Buttermilk ½ cup

Salt to taste

Cashews 8, roasted/ fried

Chopped coriander for garnishing

Shredded fresh coconut for garnishing

Dry coconut 1 tbs, shredded

Cumin seeds 1 tsp, and roasted pounded

For the tempering

Oil 1 tbs

Asafoetida (hing) 1 pinch

Turmeric 1 tsp

Mustard seeds 1 tsp

Curry leaves 6

Method

Soak rice for an hour. Measure water to twice the quantity of rice. Prepare the tempering in a pan; add Ivy gourds quarters and saute well for 3-4 minutes. Add rice and saute together. Heat the water and add to the rice-ivy gourd mixture. Cover and cook.

Once the rice softens, add the freshly prepared masala, kaala masala, salt and jaggery. Mix well and cover to steam.

Uncover and add the buttermilk. Mix well and cover again to steam.

Serve this *Masaale Bhaat* with a garnish of shredded coconut, cashews and chopped coriander. A bowl of spiced buttermilk and jilebi would complete the meal.

Note: One may substitute vegetables with aubergines to make Vaangi Bhaat.

Dahi Bhaat

Summer calls for easily digestible meals. I have memories of sweltering summer afternoons in India when all we wanted was Dahi Bhaat or Dahi Butti. *Dahi Butti* and fried *Kutachyaa Mirchya*. My maternal aunt makes *Dahi Bhaat* with pomegranate seeds, while my mother adds grated cucumber. Either way, it tastes terrific and is cooling.

Ingredients

Cooked rice 1 cup

Yogurt 1/2 cup

Milk 1/2 cup

Salt to taste

Sugar 1/2 tsp (optional)

For tempering

Green/red chillies to taste, chopped

Cumin seeds 1 tsp

Clarified butter 1 tsp

Curry leaves 4

Asafoetida a pinch

Chopped coriander for garnishing

Method

When fresh cooked rice is cool, add yogurt, salt and sugar. Prepare the tempering and add to the rice. Cover and set aside (I normally prepare this 10-15 mins in advance. This helps the yoghurt absorb the aromas of the tempering) Just before serving, add milk. Mix well. Garnish with chopped coriander.

If you do not have enough yogurt, use buttermilk. This recipe is very handy for picnics too. Just mix the cold rice with tempering and add in the yogurt and milk just before serving.

Note: I use chopped green chillies or dry red chillies broken into pieces. To add texture, add one tsp of udid dal in the tempering.

Naarali Bhaat

This rice preparation is quite simple and can be done very quickly if you have ready, grated coconut and loose jaggery. Clarified butter is the vital ingredient here. Apparently, it does bring up the flavours. Pour in a couple of tablespoons of tup before steaming the whole preparation. This rice makes the primary dish on Naarali Pournima. However, it can be relished as a dessert on any other occasion.

Ingredients

Rice 1 cup

Coconut 1/4 cup, freshly grated

Jaggery 1.5 cups

Cloves 3

Cardamom 3

Clarified butter 2 heaped tbss

Blanched almonds and/or raisins 1 tbs

Method

Wash and drain the rice. Set aside for about an hour. Heat 1 tbs of clarified butter in a pan and add cloves. Add the washed and drained rice. Roast the rice in the clarified butter for a couple of minutes till all the grains are coated and shiny. Add twice the measure of warm water to the rice and cook. The rice should be fluffy, each grain separate. In a thick bottomed pan, cook the grated coconut and jaggery together. Once the jaggery melts and softens the coconut slightly, add the cooked rice and toss together gently. Add cardamom, blanched almonds and raisins. Mix the rest of the clarified butter and fold in, taking care not to mash the rice. Cover and let it steam briefly.

This sweet rice can be served either warm or cold.

Saakhar Bhaat

Ingredients

Rice 1 cup

Sugar 1 cup

Water ½ cup

Clarified butter 2 heaped tbss

Cloves 3

Cardamom 3

Blanched almonds and or raisins 1 tbs

A few saffron strands

Method

Wash and drain the rice. Set aside for about an hour. In a pan heat sugar and water to make a sugar syrup. Add saffron when the syrup simmers and then bring it to a boil. Set aside.

Heat 1 tbs of clarified butter in a pan and add cloves and washed and drained rice. Roast the rice in the clarified butter for a couple of minutes, till all the grains are coated and shiny.

Add 1.5 measures of warm water and cook the rice. When the grains are softened, add the sugar syrup. Cover and steam. The rice must be fluffy; each grain needs to stand out. Add cardamom, blanched almonds and raisins.

Add the rest of the clarified butter and fold gently taking care not to mash the rice. Cover and let it steam briefly before serving.

Vegetables and Daals

Sangeeta Mavshi, Degloorkar Ajji and Yermalkar Ajji

Culinary Terms, Management and Alchemy

Kitchen management and cooking alchemy are very complex realms. Someone who is adept in the skill and can efficiently manage resources in the kitchen deserves accolades. One such person I hold in high esteem is Degloorkar *ajji*, Rajesh's maternal grandmother. I have seen her tiny kitchen, which has minimum yet apt resources, all placed perfectly. Her kitchen practices would result in everyday meals being prepared with no hassle and no time wasted. No guests went away without having had a cup of tea and a bowl of warm *Upma* or *Sheera* that *Ajji* would have ready by the time the visitors settled down on the foldable tin chairs and began their chat with Anna, her husband. If a child walked in to the house, there would always be a *dabba* of *Ladu*, *Vadi* or a lucky helping from a jar of *shrikhandaachya* or *limletchya golya* (assorted candies).

Cleaning and tidying the kitchen before Navratri is a common practice in every household in Maharashtra, but Degloorkar *ajji* preferred keeping her kitchen sparkling clean all year round. Her resources were well organised in clean steel and brass *dabbe* (boxes). If a *dabba* was empty and needed refilling, she would wash it, dry it and make sure it held whatever was necessary. So when the other women in the family or the neighbourhood huffed and puffed about the mega-task of *swaypak gharachi safaai* – that all-important kitchen cleaning and organising, she had no reason to fret, since it was already done.

She would recycle Forhans toothpaste cartons, cut into strips and stored in a recycled Dalda tin or a biscuit box, which perched next to the gas stove. These she'd use to light the gas or a *kandil,* rather than striking a matchstick every time. Ajji had a resource of roasted *rawa,* just a few *vaatya* (bowls) for last minute guests, thereby making sure that there was a feast of *Sheera* or *Upma* for them. She'd plan for the fortnight and keep her kitchen well stocked for meals. Jaggery was grated and saved in an airtight container with a plastic sheet under the lid to avoid moisture seeping in; peanuts roasted and crushed in the *khal batta* for the *bhaajya* and for *upaas* were packed away in separate containers; and *khau cha dabbe* were filled with *Naaralachi* or *Besanachi Vadi* and at times with *Laadu* for any children or grandchildren visiting her.

She knew what was at hand – red chilli powder, turmeric, kaalaa masala, salt, sugar, rice, wheat flour, *jwari-baajri* flour, gram flour and essential spices, along with a stash of pickle jars, dry chutneys and *Metkut* stood lined up on a rack for the effective running of *ajji's* kitchen. She kept an eagle eye on the kitchen inventory and on fresh stock, including dairy products, to help the smooth functioning of her kitchen.

The techniques included in Marathi cuisine are, broadly, roasting, frying, tempering, steaming, sauteing and boiling. Additionally, preparing the vegetables (e.g. *chochne,* or chopping cucumber fine by making incisions lengthwise and cutting across its width) and flours (*kanik timbane,* kneading flour for *polya*) and churning buttermilk (t*aak ghusalne),* steaming vegetables (*bhaaji vaafavne*) and pounding *(kutne).* Knowing the nuances of techniques and mastering them enables you to understand food and what you are trying to achieve in the kitchen.

I recall *Tai* warming up a *ghamela* (vessel) of water in her kitchen, covering it and setting it aside. She would add the warm water to the vegetables or *Aamti* to cook them or to bring the dish to the right consistency. Adding cold water would affect the core temperature of the preparation and stop cooking and the process would have to be restarted from scratch. Thus warm water is always recommended when cooking, she would say.

Susheela Kaku makes a simple yet delicious cauliflower bhaaji which is finely chopped, tempered as usual and lightly flavoured with red chilli powder and goda masala. It is slow cooked with a water lid on. *Paanyache zaakan* or water lids kept for cooking *phul-phal bhajya*. When a steam is generated inside the vessel, there is an equal distribution of heat both inside and on top of the vessel, speeding up the cooking process.

Tempering, or *phodni* in Marathi, plays a vital role in adding to the nutrient value and aroma of food. Generally, *goda tel* or *tup* (oil and clarified butter) are used to temper the seeds that give flavour. The fat, when heated, unlocks the essence of the spices used. The essential oils in the spices are sensitive to heat. Hence the oil should not be overheated or allowed to reach smoking point. Once the spices sizzle in the hot oil, the flavours and aroma are absorbed by it. To temper, the oil is heated and the spices added in sequence, depending on the time each requires to splutter and release its flavours. Cumin seeds sizzle at a lower temperature, while mustard seeds need comparatively high heat to splutter. Hence if the two are to be used together, the mustard must be added first and then, once it begins to splutter, the heat should be turned down and cumin added. Turmeric, chilli powder and *Kaalaa masala* follow in sequence and are stirred in quickly to avoid burning. This flavoursome carrier oil is ready to transform each of the ingredients being cooked.

I have been lucky to have relished meals prepared on the *chul*, the clay stove, and anyone who has tasted food cooked on the flame will remember the delicious and rustic taste this imparts. Even today, our house at Jalna has a *chul* in the backyard. The stove is lit at the break of dawn to saturate the oven for even cooking. The heat generated initially is used to make tea or boil milk. Later, the glowing embers are pushed against the walls of the *chul* to maintain the heat for the entire cooking time; consistent fuelling by wood and cowdung cakes keeps the stove at a constant heat, thus allowing slow cooking, which allows the nutrients to stay intact. Hence the meals cooked on thus taste fabulous, with beautiful flavours.

Yermalkar *Ajji*, *Tai* and Degloorkar *Ajji* prepared *Sarbarit Paale Bhaajya*, perfectly spiced and cooked to the right consistency. None of these women recorded their reasons for using one ingredient over the other in their *Kaalaa masala*. However, they are adept in the kitchen – this, together with their magical cooking skills and the knowledge of the alchemy involved, have made every *bhaaji*, whether textured with gram flour, crushed peanuts or churned with the usual tempering spices, stay fresh and delicious in their grandchildren's memories.

I follow my mother-in-law's practice of sun drying the local berries and using them to flavour leafy vegetables sides especially if one is tired of the same old tamarind in each of the preparations. E.g. jujubes are sun-dried and used in flavouring *methichi* or even *harbaryachya paalyachi bhaaji* (*young chickpea leaves*).

This section looks into various dairy products, vegetables and daal prepared in our family, hailing from the Marathwada region.

Dairy Products

Dahi (Curd/Yogurt)

The temperature conditions in India, especially in Maharashtra, are ideal for setting a thick curd. Full fat milk, an appropriate container, a starter to set the curd and warmth – these are the conditions required.

In a pan, heat milk till it is lukewarm. Meanwhile, stir the starter curd in a small bowl until there are no lumps and set aside. Pour the lukewarm milk into a container – I like setting curd in a terracotta pot. Spoon a tablespoon of lukewarm milk into the starter and mix well. Stir this dilute starter mix gently into the rest of the lukewarm milk. Cover and set aside. Ideally, when I am in India I set curd at night and it is ready in the morning during the summer.

Notes

1. The starter should not be added to hot or boiling milk. It requires milk at a lukewarm temperature.

2. Too much starter will not set the curd properly.

3. Once the curd is set, scoop out servings with a spoon – but do not leave the spoon in the curd as water will drain into the hollow created.

4. If the weather is very hot, move the container to a slightly cooler place, or else the curd will turn sour.

5. If the weather is cold, it helps to keep the container in a warm place – I put it in the oven with the oven light on.

Loni-Taak (Butter and buttermilk)

Homemade butter can be made using the cream extracted from fresh milk. I recall how every time milk was heated and then cooled, it developed a skin on the surface. This is the cream used to make butter. When the milk cools down, the vessel is placed in the fridge. I loved how the cream thickened on top of the milk. This thick cream is carefully removed and placed in another container. I start collecting it on Monday. To this first collection, I add a tablespoon of curd starter and stir well and place it in the fridge. Every time milk is heated and cooled, the thick layer of cream that develops is collected and added to the container with the starter mixed into the cream. This I continue doing till Friday.

Then comes the real adventure. Place the container with the cream collected over the week on the kitchen counter. Stir well and leave overnight.

This allows the curd to set in the cream mixture. The next morning, churn the cream-curd using a rawi (a traditional churner). Add a cup of cold water and keep churning until the butter begins to separate from the buttermilk. You can use a blender to do this.

Gently take the soft butter out of the liquid and place it in a separate dish. Add ¼ cup of water to wash this butter clean, draining off the remaining traces of buttermilk.

This clean white butter can be stored in the fridge or used to make tup (clarified butter) for the family.

Fresh homemade butter goes well with Thalipith or Dhapaate, and I love it spread on toast and sprinkled with sugar.

The leftover buttermilk is either used to make spiced Taak or cooked into Kadhi (see chapter on Sides).

Tup, Ghee or Clarified Butter

Place a pan on low heat. Add butter and let it melt. Allow this melted butter to simmer on low heat for 5-8 minutes. It begins to clarify and froth. This is an indication that the clarified butter is ready. My mother's litmus test to check the end point is to sprinkle on some water – if the water splutters and evaporates, it shows that the clarifying process is complete. Turn the heat off. Strain the golden clarified butter into a jar to cool down, leaving behind the residual solids called tupachi beri. Once it is cool, the clarified butter gains a granular texture.

Note

A betel nut leaf added as the butter clarifies will infuse the Tup with a hint of aroma and goodness.

Tupachi beri is often relished with sugar or grated jaggery. Aai makes delicious Laadu by adding roasted wheat flour to a mixture of jaggery and beri.

Vegetables and Daals

Phal bhajya like *Bataataa, Vangi, Chakri* (pumpkin), *dodke, dudhi* are mainly cooked with *chinch* *(turmeric), gul (jaggery), kaalaa masala, danyaache kut* and steamed with *paanyache zakan.*

. . . .

Bataatyaachi Bhaaji

Ingredients

Potatoes 4, boiled, peeled and diced

Green chillies 2, chopped

Curry leaves 5-6

Udid daal 1 tsp

Oil 2 tbs

Mustard seeds 1 tsp

Asafoetida 1 pinch

Turmeric 1 tsp

Lemon juice 3 tbs

Coriander ¼ cup, chopped

Sugar ½ tsp

Salt to taste

Method

Heat oil in a pan and temper with mustard seeds, Udid daal, curry leaves and asafoetida, followed by turmeric. Add green chillies, potatoes, salt and sugar. Mix well so that the oil coats the potato. Cover and cook for two minutes. Add lemon juice and mix. Garnish with chopped coriander and serve with *polya* or *purya.*

You could flavour this *bhaaji* with finely grated ginger.

Shredded fresh coconut and chopped coriander can be used to garnish.

Bataatyaachya Kaachrya

Ingredients

Potatoes 3

Oil 4 tbs

Mustard seeds ½ tsp

Cumin seeds ½ tsp

Asafoetida 1 pinch

Turmeric 1 tsp

Red chilli powder 1 tsp

Coriander ¼ cup, chopped

Sugar ½ tsp

Salt to taste

Method

This *bhaaji* requires more oil to cook the potatoes and make them crisp. Wash and peel the potatoes, cut into quarters, then into thin slices and cover with water. This will drain out some of the starch and prevent blackening of the potatoes. This water can be used to thin down the consistency of daal, pithle or even in cooking kadhi.

In a *kadhai*, heat oil. Temper with mustard seeds, followed by cumin seeds, asafoetida and turmeric. Add the drained potatoes and stir. Add red chilli powder and salt. Mix well. Cover and cook on medium heat, stirring occasionally to avoid the potatoes sticking to the bottom and sides of the pan.

Once the potatoes are cooked and crisp at the edges, garnish with shredded dry coconut and chopped coriander.

Kobichi Bhaaji

Ingredients

Cabbage 2 cups, shredded

Onion 1, finely chopped

Green chillies 2, chopped

Curry leaves 5-6

Oil 2 tbs

Mustard seeds 1 tsp

Asafoetida 1 pinch

Turmeric 1 tsp

Ginger 1 tsp, finely grated

Coriander ¼ cup, chopped

Sugar ½ tsp

Salt to taste

Method

Heat oil in a pan and temper with mustard seeds and asafoetida, followed by turmeric. Add green chillies, ginger and onions. Saute until the onions soften slightly. Add cabbage and stir well till coated with the onion mixture. Cover with water lid and cook. Season with salt, sprinkle on sugar and mix. Cover and cook for a couple of minutes. Garnish with coriander before serving.

Option: Soaked Harbaraa daal can be used to cook this vegetable. It is added to the tempering before adding the chopped kobi.

Tomato Chi Bhaaji

Ingredients

Tomatoes 4, Chopped

Green chillies 2, chopped

Curry leaves 5-6

Coriander ¼ cup

Peanuts 2 tbs, roasted and crushed

Sugar 1 tsp

Salt to taste

Mustard seeds 1 tsp

Asafoetida a pinch

Turmeric

Oil 2 tbs

Method

In a pan heat oil and temper with mustard seeds and asafoetida. Add turmeric, curry leaves and green chillies and saute for a minute. Add chopped tomatoes. Stir and cover to cook until the tomatoes soften slightly. Add sugar and salt and the crushed peanuts. Garnish with chopped coriander and serve hot.

You may use green or red tomatoes for this vegetable side.

Mudda Bhaaji

Ingredients

Methi leaves (fenugreek greens) 1 bundle, cleaned, washed and chopped

Toor daal 1 cup

Gram flour 2 tbs

Salt to taste

Oil for tempering

Mustard seeds 1 tsp

Asafoetida a pinch

Turmeric powder 1 tsp

Red chilli powder 1 tsp or to taste

Tamarind pulp 1 tsp

Jaggery 1 tsp

Further tempering

Oil 1 tbs

Mustard seeds 1 tsp

Asafoetida a pinch

Dry red chillies 2-3

Method

Temper hot oil with mustard seeds, turmeric and asafoetida. Add dal and methi together and cook until done. Use a pressure cooker if you prefer to cook both. Once cooked, mix well. In a pan roast gram flour in about half a tsp of oil. Add to it the methi and daal mix. Add salt, chilli powder, tamarind and jaggery. Cook for a couple of minutes. We like this *bhaaji* thick so only a little water is added to adjust the consistency.

An extra tempering is often added just before serving. Heat oil and add mustard seeds, asafoetida and dry red chillies. This is poured on top of the *bhaaji* and lifts it an extra notch in taste. Serve with *roti*, rice or *bhaakri*.

Gargata is another way of making green, leafy vegetables delectable. A comforting vegetable side that I like with plain rice, *Gargata* varies slightly from *Mudda bhaaji*. The *daal* is not cooked in advance, but soaked for half an hour and cooked together with chopped green leafy vegetables, spices and the gram flour mix. However, tender beans and peanuts whole or roasted and pounded coarsely – are added to the cooked vegetables.

Note: You may use green leafy vegetables like amaranth leaves, sorrels, spinach or a mix of spinach and fenugreek leaves for both *Mudda Bhaaji* and *Gargata*.

Bharli Vaangi or Vaangi Masala

Ingredients

Small aubergines 500g

Onions 2, medium, chopped (optional)

Grated dry coconut 2 tbs

Crushed peanuts 2 tbs

Kaalaa masala 2 tbs

Turmeric 1 tsp

Chilli powder 1 tsp

Mustard seeds 1 tsp

Oil 3 tbs

Asafoetida a pinch

Salt to taste

Coriander to garnish

Method

Wash the aubergines. Slit in a cross pattern to create four portions joined at the base. In a pan, temper oil with mustard seeds and asafoetida. When the mustard seeds splutter, add the turmeric. Saute the onions. Add the slit aubergines and saute for a couple of minutes. Cover and steam. When slightly softened, add chilli powder, kaalaa masala, crushed peanuts and coconut and stir. Add salt to taste and 1 cup warm water. Cover and cook. The aubergines should be softened and coated with masala. Garnish with chopped coriander and serve with *bhaakri or polya*.

Ambaadichi Bhaaji

Ingredients

Ambaadi 1 bunch

Peanuts ¼ cup

Harbaraa daal 1 cup

Garlic cloves 4, chopped

Green chillies chopped 2, chopped

Gram flour 2 tbs

Red chilli powder 1 tsp

Kaalaa Masala 1 tsp

Jaggery 1 tbs

Asafoetida 1 pinch

Oil 3 tbs

Mustard seeds 1 tsp

Salt to taste

Method

Clean and wash the ambaadi leaves. In separate pans, pressure cook harbaraa daal, and the leaves. Once cool, drain the cooked leaves in a sieve to extract as much water as possible. This will help to reduce the significant tartness the leaves otherwise impart to the preparation. Set aside. Mash the cooked harbaraa daal.

Crush garlic and green chillies together.

Heat 1tbs of oil in a pan. Roast the gram flour until it releases a nice aroma. Set the flour aside in a bowl. In the same pan, add the rest of the oil and temper with mustard seeds, asafoetida, peanuts, crushed green chillies and garlic. Saute for a couple of minutes. Add cooked ambaadi, mashed harbaraa daal and roasted gram flour. Mix red chilli powder, *kaalaa masala* and jaggery. Add half cup of water or more to get the desired consistency. Season with salt and mix well. Cook for a few minutes until the flavours blend.

A *shili* (a day old) *poli* or a *bhaakri* goes well with this *bhaaji*. My mother likes using *tandalachya kanya* in this bhaaji. Rice soaked for an hour, ground coarsely and added to the tempering along with cooked ambaadi gives it a nice texture. Jwari kani can also be used.

Usal

Usal is a kaalvan made with sprouts. When using moog or black-eyed beans, I dry roast and pressure cook them first. To sprout *matki*, you need to soak it in the morning, drain it in the afternoon and tie it into muslin and set it in a warm place. Ideally, the beans sprout in a couple of days in the summer, but need a few more days in colder weather.

Ingredients

Matki sprouted (moth beans)

Kaalaa masala 2 tsp

Green chillies 1-2

Red chilli powder (optional or instead of green chillies) to taste

Cumin seeds 1 tsp

Coconut 2 tbs

Jaggery 1 tsp

Tamarind pulp 1/2 tsp

For tempering

Oil 1tbs

Mustard seeds1 tsp

Curry leaves 4-5

Asafoetida a generous pinch

Method

Grind green chillies, coconut and cumin seeds together and set aside. Cook the sprouts – I usually pressure cook these. Add kaalaa, masala, salt, jaggery and tamarind pulp. Mix well. Temper 1 tbs oil with mustard seeds, curry leaves and asafoetida. Add this to the cooked sprouts. If you prefer thinner consistency, add a quarter cup of water and cook for 4-5 mins. Garnish with chopped coriander and serve with *Polya* or rice.

Vaangyaache Bharit

Vaangyaache bharit is prepared by roasting aubergines on fire and then mixing the flesh with spices and herbs. The mash is seasoned and tempered before serving. At times, *Bharit* is mixed with yogurt, which gives it a cooling and tangy taste.

I usually prepare this *Bharit* by pricking, oiling and roasting the aubergines on an open flame. But *Aai* (my mother) has a different and quick way of preparing it.

Ingredients

Aubergine 2

Onion 1, medium sized, chopped

Green chillies 2-3, chopped

Salt to taste

For tempering

Oil 1 tbs (to saute the aubergine)

Oil 2 tbs

Mustard seeds 1 tsp

Asafoetida a pinch

Turmeric 1 tsp

Chilli powder one tsp

Coriander for garnishing

Method

Wash and cut the aubergine into cubes. Saute in 1 tbs oil. Set aside. When cool, mash with your hands or a potato masher. In the same pan, add oil for tempering and add mustard seeds, asafoetida, turmeric and red chilli powder. Add green chillies, saute, and then add chopped onions and fry until slightly softened. Add the aubergine mash and salt to taste. Garnish with coriander and serve with hot *Polya*.

Note: Bharit means vegetable mash. Vegetables like pumpkin, capsicum are either steamed or roasted the accompaniment. *Bhopalyache bharit* is prepared by steaming pumpkin slices, mashed and mixed with yogurt. A tempering of mustard seeds, asafoetida, dry red chillies and turmeric makes a delicious pumpkin mash

Bharli Karlyaachi Bhaaji

Stuffing vegetables like bitter gourd and ridge gourd these with masala peps up the dish and makes these gourds delicious.

Ingredients

Bitter gourd 4

Peanuts roasted and crushed, 1 cup

Kaalaa masala 1 tbs

Red chilli powder 1 tsp

Jaggery 2 tsp

Tamarind pulp 1 tbs

Oil 3 tbs

Cumin seeds

Mustard seeds 1 tsp

Turmeric 1 tsp

Asafoetida 1 pinch

Salt to taste

Method

Peel the bitter gourds and save the skin to use in the filling. discard the ends and cut the gourds into two or three equal parts. Deseed them using a spoon. Place the pieces in a pan with water and 1 tsp of salt. Boil and drain the gourds.

To make the filling

Heat 1 tbs oil and temper with cumin seeds, asafoetida and turmeric. Add peanuts, the gourd peel, Kaalaa masala, jaggery, ½ tsp salt and chilli powder and tamarind pulp. Mix well.

Fill each piece of gourd with the prepared stuffing. Save the remaining filling.

In the same pan, temper the rest of the oil with mustard seeds and turmeric. Place each of the stuffed gourd pieces in the pan, add the remaining filling and ¼ cup water. Place *paanyache zaakan* (a lid with ½ cup of water on top) and turn the heat to medium – this arrangement helps keep the vegetables moist inside the pan and prevents burning. Cook for 4-5 minutes, stirring carefully to avoid breaking the gourd pieces, until soft.

Garnish with chopped coriander and serve.

Dudhichi Bhaaji

Ingredients

Bottle gourd (*dudhi*) 1 medium sized, washed, trimmed and cubed

Harbaraa ½ cup, soaked in warm water for half an hour

Green chillies 2, chopped

Oil 1 tbs

Asafoetida a pinch

Turmeric 1 tsp

Mustard seeds 1 tsp

Water ¼ cup

Salt to taste

Method

Heat oil in a pan and temper with mustard seeds, asafoetida and add turmeric. Drain water from harbaraa daal. Add 2 tbs the water to the tempered oil and spices, cover and cook for 3-4 minutes on a low flame. Uncover and add chopped *dudhi* and salt and mix well. Pour in the rest of the water. Place a *paanyache zaakan* and cook on medium heat until the *daal* and *dudhi* are soft but not mushy.

Kaka, my father-in-law, enjoys this *bhaaji* with a dash of lemon juice. It is a smart way to add both flavour and nutrition.

Roasted peanuts instead of harbaraa can be used. A hint of red chilli powder and Kaalaa masala adds a lovely flavour to this otherwise plain dish. The method used is similar to making *Gavaarichi Bhaaji*.

Gavaarichi Bhaaji

French beans, *vaal* and cluster beans are steamed soft, roasted, crushed peanuts in this bhaaji add a little extra texture to the bhaaji. One can substitute cluster beans with any other beans of choice to make this bhaaji.

Ingredients

Cluster beans 2 cups, washed and trimmed

Peanuts ¼ cup, roasted and crushed

Oil 1 tbs

Asafoetida

Turmeric 1 tsp

Kaalaa masala 1 tsp

Mustard seeds 1 tsp

Water ¼ cup

Salt to taste

Method

Heat oil in a pan and temper with mustard seeds, asafoetida and turmeric. Add the cluster beans. Add water, cover and cook for 3-4 minutes on a low flame. Uncover and add red chilli powder, Kaalaa masala, peanuts and salt and mix well. Add water lid and cook on medium heat until the beans are soft.

Dhabbu Mirchi Chi Peeth Perun Bhaaji

Peeth ghalun or *perun* is a technique prevalent in Marathi cuisine. Onions, green leafy vegetables, drumsticks radish and cucumber are often prepared using this technique. Using *thalipith bhaajni* or *chakli bhaajni* instead of gram flour gives this *bhaaji* a rich, nutty flavour.

Ingredients

Green capsicum 4 cups, washed, deseeded and chopped finely

Oil 3 tbs

Mustard seeds 1 tsp

Asafoetida 1 pinch

Turmeric 1 tsp

Red chilli powder 1 tsp

Gram flour ¾ cup

Salt to taste

Method

Heat oil And temper with mustard seeds, asafoetida and turmeric. Add chopped capsicum and stir. Cover and cook for a couple of minutes. Uncover and add red chilli powder, salt and gram flour; mix well to coat the capsicum in the flour.

Place a *paanyache zaakan* on top and cook for a couple of minutes. Uncover and sprinkle in water to generate steam to accelerate cooking. Cover and cook till done.

Mulyaachi Bhaaji

Ingredients

Radish 2 cups, washed, peeled and chopped into cubes (use the leaves too if they are fresh and whole) Oil 2 tsps

Mustard seeds 1 tsp

Asafoetida a pinch

Turmeric 1 tsp

Green chillies 2, slit

Moog daal ¼ cup, soaked in water for half an hour Salt to taste

Sugar 1/2 tsp

You could use roasted crushed peanuts instead of moog daal.

Method

Temper hot oil with mustard seeds, asafoetida and turmeric and green chillies. Saute for a couple of minutes and add moog daal. Add 2 tbs of water, cover and cook for 3 minutes. Add chopped radish and the leaves; add salt, sugar and mix well. Place a *paanyache zaakan* on top and cook for another 3 minutes. Radishes soften very quickly, so be vigilant to avoid the vegetable becoming mushy.

. . . .

Shepuchi Bhaaji

Ingredients

Shepu (fresh dill) 2 cups, sorted and chopped roughly

Green chillies 2, chopped roughly

Moong daal 1/2 cup, soaked in water for half an hour or peanuts, roasted and crushed

Oil 2wo tsp

Water 1 cup

Salt and sugar to taste

Method

In a pan heat oil. Add green chillies and stir. Add chopped dill and stir for a few minutes. Add salt and a sprinkle of sugar, along with just enough water to cook the dal. Add washed daal to the boiling liquid and cook till soft.

Serve hot with hot *polya*.

Bhendichi Bhaaji

Ingredients

Bhendi (okra) 250g

Green chillies 2, slit, (or red chilli powder 1 tsp)

Curry leaves 5-6

Coriander ¼ cup

Peanuts 2 tbs, roasted and crushed

Juice of half a lemon

Salt to taste

Mustard seeds 1 tsp

Asafoetida a pinch

Turmeric

Oil 3 tbs

Wash and dry bhendi. Chop into roundels.

Method

In a pan heat oil and temper with mustard seeds and asafoetida. Add turmeric, curry leaves and green chillies and saute for a minute. Add chopped bhendi and cook for a couple of minutes. Add lemon juice and stir. Adding lemon juice avoids the *bhaaji* getting sticky. Keep the heat on low and keep stirring. Add sugar and salt. Add the crushed peanuts and cook until the bhaaji is cooked and crisp. Garnish with chopped coriander and serve hot.

Daal Bhaaji

This is a quick one-pot dish that can be made more interesting with vegetables like aubergine, fenugreek leaves and ridge gourd. Daal bhaaji goes well with rice, *polya* or *bhakri*.

Ingredients

Toor daal 1 cup

Aubergine I large, cubed or any other vegetable of your choice

Mustard seeds 1 tsp

Red chilli powder 2 tsp

Kaalaa masala 2 tsp

Jaggery 1 tbs

Tamarind pulp 1 tsp

Curry leaves 4

Salt to taste

Chopped coriander for garnishing

Method

Pressure cook the daal until soft. In a separate pan, temper oil with mustard seeds and curry leaves. Steam the aubergine cubes till soft. Add the softened daal, followed by chilli powder, Kaalaa masala, jaggery and tamarind pulp. Simmer briefly and garnish with chopped coriander. Add water if you want a thinner consistency.

Saadha Varan

Saadha Varan, *tup*, *bhaat* and a dash of lemon evokes many memories of comforting meals.

Ingredients

Toor daal 1 cup

Turmeric ½ tsp

Asafoetida a pinch

Sugar or jaggery ½ tsp

Salt to taste

Method

Pressure cook toor daal with turmeric. Mash the daal and add 1/2 cup water. Add salt, asafoetida and sugar/jaggery. Bring to a quick boil and serve on a heap of piping hot rice with a dollop of clarified butter (*tup*). A dash of lemon juice will raise it to another level!

Variation : Ghatta Varan

Saadha Varan when cooked and mashed can either be used for *Aamti* or made into a quick accompaniment of *Ghatta Varan*. A generous tempering of chopped garlic, Kaalaa masala and seasoning is a quick solution to a meal shy of accompaniments. It can further be spiced up with a handful of chopped onion and raw mango.

Chinch Gulaachi Aamti

Tai and Radhika *mami's Chinch Gulachi Aamti* is devoured by everyone in the family. Children who disliked vegetables found it a huge relief to have a bowl of *aamti* on the table.

Ingredients

Toor daal 1 cup

Turmeric ½ tsp

Asafoetida a pinch

Oil for tempering

Mustard seeds 1 tsp

Kaalaa masala 2 tsp

Jaggery 2 tsp, grated

Tamarind pulp 1 tsp

Curry leaves – 8-9

Coriander for garnishing

Salt to taste

Water 1 cup or more

Method

Pressure cook daal with turmeric and mash. Add salt and tamarind pulp, jaggery and spices. In a pan temper oil with mustard seeds, asafoetida and curry leaves. To this add the daal. Add water to get the desired consistency. Bring to boil. Garnish with chopped coriander leaves.

Aamti: To make *aamti*, you could use any kind variety of daal, e.g. toor, moong, masoor, harbaraa. Instead of flavouring with chinch-gul, adding phal bhaajya, shenga (drumsticks) makes a distinct aamti.

Yessar Pithi

Yessar is a versatile mix is a useful resource in the kitchen! Coarsely ground daals may be mixed with *Metkut* and yogurt to make a last minute *Daangar*-like preparation, or tempered with oil or mixed in *kaccha tel* for a quick accompaniment. *Yessar* adds a unique taste and nutritional value to gravies. When mixed with spices and chopped coriander it makes faux *Golyanchi Aamti* and the *pithi* is a good thickener as well. Yessar pithi is given to a groom's family after the wedding ceremony, so that the family can have a meal either on their way home with *bhaaji*, *polya* and *tel*, or can prepare one when they get home.

Ingredients

To make the Yessar mix

Harbaraa daal ½ cup

Udid daal ¼ cup

Moong daal ¼ cup

Coriander 1 tbs

Cumin 1/2 tbs

Metkut 4 tbs

To make golyanchi amti

Yessar mix 4 tbs

Metkut 1 tbs

Red chilli powder 1 tsp

Turmeric 1 tsp

Salt to taste

Asafoetida a pinch

Chopped coriander a sprig

Water to make the dough balls ¼ cup or less

Other Ingredients

Onion 1, finely chopped

Dry coconut 1 tbs, grated and roasted

Garlic cloves 2

Tamarind pulp 1 tbs

Jaggery ½ tbs

Asafoetida a pinch

Turmeric 1 tsp

Kaalaa masala 1 tsp

Oil 1 tsp

Mustard seeds

Water 1.5 cups

Yessar pithi 1 tbs to thicken the gravy

Method

Dry roast each ingredient separately . Cool slightly and grind to a fine powder.

In a bowl, mix dough and make small sized balls. Set aside.

Grind onion, garlic and dry coconut to a fine paste. Add a little water if needed, only to bring the mix together.

PAAT PAANI

In a pan temper oil with mustard seeds and asafoetida. Add the onion-garlic mix and saute. Add turmeric, asafoetida and Kaalaa masala and mix well. Pour in 1.3 cups water and bring to a simmer. Add salt, tamarind, jaggery and *Yessar Pithi*. Add the dough balls gently into the simmering aamti and bring to a boil. Once completely cooked, garnish with chopped coriander.

Serve hot with rice, *bhakri* or *polya*.

Purnachi Amti

Ingredients

Harbaraa daal 1 cup

Turmeric ½ tsp

Asafoetida a pinch

Oil for tempering

Mustard seeds 1 tsp

Kaalaa masala 2 tsp

Jaggery 2 tsp, grated

Tamarind pulp 1 tsp

Curry leaves 8-9

Coriander for garnishing

Salt to taste

Water 2 cups for pressure cooking and more for the *aamti*

Method

Pressure cook daal with turmeric. Drain in a sieve and collect the drained liquid. To this add salt and tamarind pulp, jaggery and spices. In a pan temper mustard seeds in oil with asafoetida and curry leaves. Add the drained liquid mix. Add water to get the desired consistency. Bring to a boil. Garnish with chopped coriander leaves.

. . . .

Daalichya Pithache Pithle

Ingredients

Gram flour ½ cup

Green chillies 2 (or to taste)

Mustard seeds 1 tsp

Salt

Fresh coriander leaves for garnishing (optional)

Water 4 cups, boiling hot

Oil 1 tsp

Asafoetida 1 pinch

Turmeric ½ tsp

Onions and garlic can be added

Method

In a kadhai, temper hot oilwith mustard seeds, asafoetida and chopped green chillies. Add 4 cups of boiling water and salt. Now is the tricky part: Add gram flour in small portions and keep mixing to avoid lumps. Let this cook until the raw taste is gone and garnish with coriander. The consistency of the *pithle* can be varied by adding water.

Saar

Ingredients

Thick tamarind pulp 2 tbs

Tup 1/2 tsp

Cumin seeds 1/4 tsp

Red chilli powder 1 tsp

Curry leaves 4-5

Salt to taste

Jaggery 1 tsp or more to balance the sweet and sour tastes

Water 4 cups

Chopped coriander for garnishing

Method

In a pan, temper tup with cumin. Add the tamarind pulp and water. Bring to a boil. Add salt and jaggery to make a balanced tangy-sweet thin soup.

Garnish with chopped coriander and serve piping hot with *khichadi* or just pour into a cup and sip.

You can make *Saar* using tomatoes or raw mango. For Tomato Saar, peel and puree tomatoes in and add to the flavoured water. Or boil or grate raw mango into the liquid. My mother uses the seeds of raw mango to make this, once the rest of the unripe fruit is used to make chutney or *methamba*. The seeds impart a tart flavour. *Yessar Pithi* is often used to thicken saar and add flavour.

Kadhi

Ingredients

Gram flour 1 tbs

Buttermilk 1 cup

Cumin seeds ½ tsp

Green chilli 1

Garlic clove 1

Ginger ½ inch

Curry leaves 4-5

Salt

Sugar ½ tsp

For tempering

Tup (or oil) 2 tsp

Mustard seeds ½ tsp

Cumin seeds ½ tsp

Asafoetida 1 pinch

Turmeric 1/2 tsp

Method

Crush cumin seeds, ginger, garlic and green chilli. To this add Gram flour, salt, sugar and a little buttermilk. Blend well and gradually mix in the rest of the buttermilk.

Heat a pan and temper hot tup with mustard seeds, cumin seeds, curry leaves and turmeric. This needs to be done quickly to prevent the clarified butter burning. Alternatively, temper using oil and add a dollop of tup to the *Kadhi* when cooked.

Add the flavoured buttermilk mixture. Gram flour will help stabilise it and stop the buttermilk splitting. Keep stirring on low heat until it boils.

Garnish with chopped coriander and serve with *polya* or *bhaat*.

Kadhi, saadha varan-bhaat and *tup* is my comfort food.

Vaatli Daal

Ingredients

Harbaraa daal 1 cup, soaked for a couple of hours and drained

Raw mango 1/4 cup, grated

Oil 1 tsp

Mustard 1 tsp

Curry leaves 4-5

Asafoetida a pinch

Turmeric 1 tsp

Green chillies 2, chopped

Red chillies 2

Salt to taste

Sugar ½ tsp

Chopped coriander to garnish

Fresh shredded coconut to garnish

Method

Grind the soaked and drained daal roughly and set aside.

In a thick bottomed pan temper oil with mustard seeds, asafoetida and curry leaves. Add 1tsp turmeric and the roughly ground dal. Stir and cover. Cook for 4-5 mins. Add salt and sugar. Stir again, cover and cook. Add grated mango and mix. The daal should be cooked until the raw taste is gone. Transfer the daal to a bowl, garnish with coriander leaves and shredded coconut. Serve either warm with a meal or cold as a snack.

Breads

Deo Ajji

The Milling Stone and
Our Pantry

Customary breads featured in this cuisine are mainly flatbreads, including *bhakri*, *poli*, *dhapaate dashmi*, *puri* and *thaalipith*. Variations come into play when these unleavened breads are either rolled flat or stuffed; some are fried or even steamed. Flatbreads like *thaalipith*, *bhaakri* and *dhapaate* are patted flat between the palms, while others are rolled out. Each is paired with *kaalvan* sides to enhance the eating experience. A regular Marathi meal includes *Polya* or at times *Ghadichya Polya*, with sides of vegetables and lentils.

The *Kankecha dabaa* is quintessentially part of a Marathi pantry – it holds a supply of wheat flour sufficient for the family for about a month. The wheat is milled at the local *girni* (grinding mills) for everyday use. I recall as a child, it was a monthly ritual assisting either Aai or Baba take the grain to the milling centre, where people would gather around or sit on the wooden benches set outside and wait their turn. Those in a hurry were asked to come back later or leave their bag of grains to be ground in due course, to be collected when done. The *girni-wala* operator was given instructions about the stage to which the grains needed milling. Such mills exist even today, equipped to process *bharad* or *jaad*, *bareek* and *sapeet* for multiple uses in the kitchen.

On one visit to Nidhona village, from where Deo family hails, I had the privilege of visiting the house, my mother-in-law had stepped into as a bride. The baithak or living room walls were untouched by commercial primers and paints. The kitchen was built at the left. Dense rays of sunlight pouring through the single window reflected the *shenaane saarawlele* kitchen floor. *Shen saarawne* is the ancient practice of re-surfacing floors and walls by smearing on a mixture of mud and cowdung. This allows the house to get a quick and regular make-over and the application kept the rooms warm during winter, also working as an insect repellent. Major cooking activities were carried out in the available daylight, while the evening breads were patted or rolled in the mellow illumination of the *chimney*, a lamp made with a metal container holding fuel burned with a cotton wick, or at times a *kandil* which is a lantern – if the family had enough kerosene.

The *kothighar* or pantry was at the end of the kitchen, usually pitch dark. The floors were coated with cow-dung. Aai spoke of visiting the humongous *kothya* – large metal containers that held grains and pulses – to collect supplies every time she cooked. If the resources for the day were not selected in advance or if she didn't have the time to light a *chimney* or *kandil*, the only way to identify the grains she needed was to feel them with her fingers, because it was impossible to see anything in the darkness of the *kothighar*! This was also where the *baalantin*, a new mother and her baby were encouraged to move to, quiet and warm, ideal for postnatal care. After a period of a month and a quarter, which allowed time for the new mother to regain strength and health and the baby was guarded against infections, they could get back to a routine with the rest of the family, after a visit to the temple.

Deo Aai also mentioned about an area where *jaate*, the traditional milling stone that was placed in an open area. It was used to process grains into different stages of flour. Grinding the flour needed for the day was the first ritual for the ladies of the house. Each kind of a flatbread requires *dalan*, flour processed to a different granular size. *Kanik, bharad, rawa, sapeet* (ranging from coarse to fine) was needed for the variety of breads and the recipes that required flour for either binding or for texture. While the women toiled early in the morning, they sang beautifully composed couplets, or *Jaatyavarchya ovya*, expressing their emotions. These verses conveyed their thoughts on a variety of subjects they dealt with in their everyday lives, and worked as a constructive distraction from all the hardship they faced. I tried putting together some words for Ovi that go something like this:

"As we grind lentils, wheat and rice,
Come, let us listen to the melody that the milling stones devise."

Polya

Polya is unleavened flatbread, which makes an essential part of the meal. If the dough is kneaded well, it is easy to roll out soft *polya* or *chapaati*. I recall talking with my cousin Anuya about the skilled ladies in the family – she spoke of Tai *ajji's ghadichya polya*. Tai would rotate her *poli* as she rolled each one flat, round and even. Not once did she use her hand to turn the bread while rolling it out. She made smaller *poli* than the others, yet each one fluffed up beautifully and would have multiple layers inside. She would deflate the bread and push the steam out by clapping the *poli* in the air with both hands. She then tore it into *ardhi* (half) and then *chatkor* (quarter) before serving. Aai's (my mother) *polya* are the thinnest in the family, much like the *rumali roti* served up in the North of India.

Ingredients

Kanik (whole wheat flour) 2 cups plus a little for dusting

Salt ½ tsp

Oil 2 tsp for kneading plus a little for roasting

Water ½ cup (may vary depending on the flour used)

Method

Mix flour, salt and 1 teaspoon of oil. Add water gradually and knead into a soft, pliable dough. Use another teaspoon of oil and knead again. Cover and set aside for at least ten minutes. Divide the dough into equal portions and roll into smooth balls. These are now ready to be rolled flat into soft *Polya*.

Heat a *tawa* (flat pan). Hold your palm slightly above the pan – if you can feel the heat, the pan is ready to roast the bread. Turn the heat to medium to cook the *Polya*. If the pan cools, turn the heat up and bring it back to the right temperature.

Dust some flour onto the *polpaat* or any flat surface. Roll a ball of dough out into a circle using gentle pressure on the rolling pin. Grease with some oil. Fold the disc in half and then half again into a quarter-shape.

Generously dust the layered triangle of dough with flour. Roll using light pressure into a circle.

Place the flatbread on the hot pan. Give it about half a minute before turning over and roast for half a minute. Flip again and apply gentle pressure on it to allow steam to build between the layers of the bread. Once it puffs up, take it off the heat and add a little ghee or oil if you prefer.

There was always a tiny portion of dough left over once the *polya* were rolled out for the main meal. Tai would either make a tiny *poli* or leave the dough and any dusting flour left over, in water till it dissolved to make a thin batter. A hint of asafoetida, chilli powder, turmeric and salt was all she added to the batter. This went on the hot tawa on which she had roasted *polya*. Her grandchildren awaited the sizzle the batter made as it hit the hot pan. Once cooked, this *lushlushit dhirde* (soft, savoury pancake) was savoured by the little ones!

Note: When *polya* dough is made using milk, the breads are called *Dashmya*. These flatbreads are an essential travel-pack food, because they have a longer shelf life.

Puri

Puri is bread that is deep fried in oil and served on special occasions. It is usually eaten with *batata bhaaji* or desserts like *kheer, aamras* or *shrikhand*.

Families in Marathwada, celebrate *Akhad* during the *Ashaadh* month which corresponds to June and July in the Gregorian calendar, with *Akhad Talne* which is fried fare. The ritual ties in with the fact that procuring dry wood for cooking was tricky due to heavy rain during this time. The women fried breads of different kinds, including *purya, tikhat mithachya purya, fulora* and *karanji* to stretch food stores until the wood dried enough for use. The advent of gas-fuelled stoves in homes has done away with this ritual in many regions. However, *akhad talne* is still a custom in our family, mainly because everyone enjoys the fried breads!

Ingredients

Kanik (whole wheat flour) 1 cup plus a little for rolling

Salt ½ tsp

Mohan (hot oil) 1 tsp

Oil for kneading 1 tsp

Water ½ cup (may vary depending on the flour used)

Oil for frying

Method

To flour and salt add hot oil (mohan). Mix well. Add water slowly and knead into a soft, pliable dough. Using another teaspoon of oil, knead well. Cover and set aside for at least ten minutes. Divide the dough into small, equal portions and roll into smooth balls. Set aside to be rolled flat into *purya*.

Pour oil into a *kadhai* or deep pan. Heat the oil to medium-high. Drop a tiny piece of dough in to check if the oil is hot enough. If the dough rises to the surface, it is ready.

Spread some flour on the *polpaat* or a flat surface. Roll a dough ball into a small disc using gentle pressure.

114

Gently slide the dough disc into the hot oil. With a slotted spoon, splash hot oil on the puri. It will begin to puff up. Flip it over in the oil and fry until golden brown.

Drain on a paper towel and make the rest of the *purya* in the same way.

Frying continuously can bring down the temperature of the oil. To make sure it is at the right temperature for each batch or *purya*, take a break and heat the oil once again to reach the desired temperature.

Serve the *purya* hot with *rassa bhaaji*, *batata bhaaji*, yogurt dips, chutney or pickles.

Tikhat Mithaachya Purya

Sudha *atya* would ritualistically pack these fried breads as a care package for those who travelled away from home, especially after a summer break at her place. It was a visual treat to see a stack of these savoury *puris* with a generous helping of *lonche* or *daanyachi chutney* packed into the last puri. When unfolded for lunch, the sadness of leaving home would be soothed.

Ingredients

Kanik (whole wheat flour) 1 cup

Gram flour 1 tbs

Rice flour 1 tbs

Asafoetida 1 pinch

Coriander powder 1 tbs

Cumin powder 1/2 tbs

Red chilli powder 1/2 tsp or to taste

Salt to taste

Mohan (hot oil) 1 tsp

Oil for kneading 1 tsp

Water ½ cup (may vary depending on the flour used)

Oil for frying

Method

In a bowl mix flour with the other dry ingredients; Add hot oil, or mohan. Mix well. Add water slowly and knead into a soft, pliable dough. Use another teaspoon of oil and knead well. Cover and set aside for at least ten minutes. Divide the dough into equal portions and roll into smooth balls. These now are ready to be rolled flat into *purya*.

Pour oil into a *kadhai* or deep pan and heat. Drop a tiny piece of dough in to check if the oil is ready to fry. If the dough rises to the top, the oil is hot enough.

Spread some flour on the *polpaat* or a flat surface. Roll a dough ball into a flat disc using gentle pressure.

Gently slide the *puri* into the hot oil. As it sizzles, with a slotted spoon splash hot oil from the kadhai on the *puri*. It will begin to puff up. Flip it over in the oil and fry until golden brown.

Drain on a paper towel and continue rolling and frying the rest of the *purya*.

Serve hot with yogurt dips, chutney or pickles.

Bhaakri

Bhakri is a flatbread made by patting the dough flat. Sorghum flour or pearl millets make gluten free flatbreads; paired with vegetable sides make a stomach-friendly meal.

Ingredients

Sorghum (jwari) flour or pearl millet (baajri) flour 1 cup

Hot water 1 cup

Salt ½ tsp

Clarified butter

Method

In a flat pan or *paraat*, mix the flour and salt. Make a well in the middle and slowly pour hot water into it. Bring the flour into the well from the sides and knead into a soft, pliable dough. Divide this dough into 2-3 equal portions.

Heat a flat pan or *tawa*. Keep a bowl of warm water handy.

Dust some flour on a *polpaat* or a flat surface. I prefer using a small *paraat* or a lipped-plate that has high edges – this allows me to pat out a circular *bhaakri*. Place a dough ball in the centre and begin patting it flat gently in a clockwise direction, helping the dough form a uniformly thin disc.

Place the *bhaakri* on the heated tawa, flour side up. Sprinkle warm water uniformly on the top – this allows the *bhaakri* to cook evenly without cracking and also forms a *paapudra* (a thin top layer). Once the water evaporates, free the *bhaakri* off the pan using a spatula and turn it over. Give it half a minute to roast on this side and move it to an open flame. Cooking on flames helps it puff up and adds to the rustic, smoky taste of these gluten-free breads. Once roasted well, serve with a dollop of clarified butter along with *rassa bhaaji* or *pithle*.

I love *bhaakri* sprinkling of salt on it.

Vaafechi Poli

When the mango, the king of fruits, makes a grand entry into the Indian markets, *Vaafechi Poli* and *Aamras* is a treat that our family eagerly awaits. Aishwarya, my talented niece, talks about the annual feast they have at Aurangabad when the mangoes are in abundance. *Aamras* is relished with these steamed breads.

Ingredients

Kanik (whole wheat flour) 1 cup

Fine semolina 1 tbs

Salt ½ tsp

Oil 2 tsp for kneading

Oil for spreading

Salt for sprinkling

Water ½ cup (may vary depending on the flour used)

Method

Mix flour, semolina, salt and 1 teaspoon of oil. Add water slowly and knead into a soft, pliable dough. Add another teaspoon of oil and knead well. Cover and set aside for at least ten minutes. Divide the dough into equal portions and roll into smooth balls.

Ideally, no dusting of flour is needed to roll out this *polya*. On a *polpaat* or a flat surface, roll out a dough ball out into a disc using gentle pressure. Grease the disc with some oil and sprinkle with salt. Fold the disc in half and then into half again.

Boil water in a pan and tie a muslin cloth on it, or set up a steamer. If water begins evaporating during cooking, add more water and let it boil and then continue the process.

Place the quarter-folded *polya* on the steamer and cook for 5-8 minutes or until done. The steamed bread should not taste raw. Place the folded flatbreads on the steamer only when the water is boiling.

Once done, separate each layer of the *polya* while the bread is still hot.

Serve with *Aamras* (mango pulp), *thecha*, chutney or pickle.

Ukhrya

Ukhrya which I learned from Arundhati, are folded breads part roasted on the *tawa* and then on embers. These are served with a generous sprinkling of *pithi saakhar*, or powdered sugar. For those who prefer savoury food, chutney, *bhurka*, pickle or *thecha* works as well.

Ingredients

Kanik (whole wheat flour) 2 cups, plus a little for rolling

Salt ½ tsp

Oil 2 tsp for kneading, plus a little for rolling

Oil for cooking

Water ½ cup (may vary depending on the flour used)

Method

Mix flour, salt and 1 teaspoon of oil. Add water slowly and knead into a soft, pliable dough. Add another teaspoon of oil and knead well. Cover and set aside for at least ten minutes. Divide the dough into equal portions and roll into smooth balls.

Heat a tawa (flat pan). To check if the pan is hot enough, hold your palm slightly above the pan. If you can feel the heat, the pan is ready for roasting the bread. Turn the heat to medium and cook the *polya* on a medium flame. If the pan cools in the process, turn the heat up and bring it back to the right temperature.

You need a mesh to roast these breads on the flame or you can hold them using tongs; however, you need to take care not to break them while doing so.

Dust some flour on a *polpaat* or a flat surface. Roll a dough ball out into a disc using gentle pressure. Grease the disc with a generous amount of oil. Fold the disc in half and grease with oil once again. Fold once again, thus making a quarter fold.

Place the folded bread on the hot pan. Give it about half a minute before turning it over and roasting for a short while. Move it to the mesh placed on the flame till cooked well.

Poke holes into the bread and allow dollops of clarified butter to seep in.

These can either be savoured with *thecha* or *bhurka* and for someone with a sweet tooth, a generous sprinkling of *pithi saakhar* (powdered sugar) or jaggery makes it an excellent source of energy.

Puran Poli

Ingredients

Filling

Harbaraa daal 3 cups washed and pressure cooked

Grated jaggery 1 ½ cups

Nutmeg powder 1/2 tsp

Cardamom powder 1/2 tsp

Few strands of saffron.

Dough

Prepare a pliable dough using the following ingredients. Set aside.

Wheat flour 3 cups

Plain flour 3 cups

Salt 1 tsp

Turmeric 1 tsp

Oil/ghee 2 tbs to make the dough smooth

Rice flour for rolling the polis ¼ cup

Method

For the covering

Mix and prepare dough softer than regular *polya* dough and set aside.

For Puran

Once the daal is pressure cooked, drain it and save the stock. This stock is used for *purnachi Aamti*. Make sure that the daal is as dry as you can manage, cool and soft (it should mash when you press it between your fingers). Transfer the daal to a heavy pan. Add the jaggery and cook this mixture over medium heat, stirring continuously. The mixture will soften and gain a reddish-brown colour. Cook till the daal and jaggery are completely mixed and the mixture comes together into a ball, this process is referred as *chatkaa dene*. Add the cardamom powder, saffron and nutmeg powder. Mix well. Turn the heat off and cool the mixture.

Rolling and filling

Place a tawa on the heat to roast the *polis*. Roll the prepared dough into a small disc. Place a ball of *Puran*, or filling, in the centre. Bring the edges together so that the *Puran* is completely covered with the dough. Dust the flat surface with rice flour and roll the prepared filled dough ball lightly. This can be tricky, as the *Puran* tends to ooze out and can burn on the pan when roasting. But practice makes perfect!

Roast the *poli* on the *tawa*. Flip over gently when one side is lightly brown, and roast the other side. Smear ghee on the cooked *Puran Poli*.

In Marathwada *Puran Poli* which are made on auspicious occasions especially kulachaar, Dassra or even on someone's birthday and is served with *purnachi Aamti*.

....

Laaturi Dhapaate

Ingredients

Fenugreek leaves 1 cup

Sorghum flour 1 cup

Gram flour ¼ cup

Coriander powder 1 tsp

Cumin powder 1 tsp

Ginger paste 1 tsp

Garlic paste 1 tsp

Turmeric 1 tsp

Red chilli powder tsp

Asafoetida a pinch

Sesame seeds 1 tsp

Carom seeds 1 tsp

Oil to roast *dhapaate*

Salt to taste

Water to make a very soft dough ¾ cup

Method

Clean the fenugreek leaves, chop and wash thoroughly. Mix all the dry ingredients in a bowl. Add the ginger-garlic paste and fenugreek leaves and mix well. Using just enough water, make a soft dough. Wet a cloth and lay it out on the kitchen counter. Grease your palm with oil. Take a small portion of the dough And place it on the cloth. Start patting the dough into a small roundel. Transfer the dough disc on to the hot pan. If you are making large *dhapaate*, make small holes in the flat disc and add a few drops of oil through the holes and along the sides while cooking. Cover and let it cook for a couple of minutes. Flip to the other side and cook until done.

Serve these multigrain *dhapaate* with chutney or pickle, or plain yogurt if you don't fancy anything piquant.

Gulachi Poli

Gulachi Poli is traditionally made during Sankranti. Jaggery and sesame in the filling provide the warmth that the body needs during the cold season.

Ingredients

For the covering

Whole wheat flour 3 cups

Plain four 1 cup

Gram flour ½ cup

Rice flour ¼ cup

Oil 2 tbs

Salt ½ tsp

Water to make a tight dough

Rice flour 1cup for dusting when rolling

To knead the dough, mix all the dry ingredients and pour in heated oil (mohan). Adding mohan makes *Gul Poli* crisp. Make a tight yet pliable dough by adding a little water. Cover and set aside for half an hour.

For the filling

Gram flour 1 cup

Sesame seeds 1 cup

Poppy seeds 1 tbs

Cardamom powder 1 tsp

Jaggery 2 cups, grated

Oil ¼ cup

Method

Roast sesame seeds and poppy seeds lightly. Grind and set aside.

Heat oil in a pan and add gram flour. Roast the gram flour until it gives off a sweet aroma and turns light pink.

In a bowl mix together roasted gram flour, jaggery, crushed sesame seeds, poppy seeds and cardamom powder. Roll into small balls and set aside.

To make the stuffed bread: Make small balls with the flour dough. Between two balls of dough, place a ball of filling. Place this assembly on a rice flour-dusted flat surface. Using a rolling pin, flatten the *poli* gently into a disc, making sure that the filling spreads to the edge evenly.

Roast on a *tawa* on medium heat.

Serve *Gul Poli* with *tup*.

Fulora

Ingredients

Plain flour 1 cup

Whole wheat flour ½ cup

Pinch of salt

Mohan (hot oil) 1 tbs

Water to knead the dough

Plain flour for dusting

Oil for frying

For filling

Make *Sheera* (as mentioned in the desserts chapter) using the following Ingredients

Semolina 1 cup

Sugar ¾ cup

Clarified butter ¼ cup

Cardamom powder ½ tsp

Method

Knead the dough, cover and set aside for half an hour.

Make small balls with the dough. Dust flour on the rolling surface. Roll out a ball of dough lightly into a fat flat disc. Place a couple of teaspoons of *sheera* on the flattened dough circle. Bring the edges of the disc together, seal and roll into a ball enclosing the filling. Roll out gently into small roundels.

Roast each roundel lightly on both sides until golden. These are delicious. However, frying them makes them taste all the more better! In a deep pan, heat oil. Slide each of the roasted, stuffed *Fulora* one at a time into the hot oil. Fry them until they turn golden-brown and drain on paper towels.

These are savoured both hot or cold. Traditionally, *Fulora* is offered as *naivedya* to the deity during Navratri celebrations. It is tied on a string as an offering, and then distributed as prasad to members of the family on Dasara, the tenth day.

Thaalipith

Deo *aaji* was a tall lady. She would perch on the kitchen platform with her left leg folded and the right touching the floor, to cook the family meals. She always sat in this way, whether it was on a chair or on the kitchen platform. Rajesh and his siblings remember their *aaji* making *Thaalipith* for her grandchildren to keep them busy until the main meal was ready. *Aaji* would pat out a gigantic *Thaalipith* referred to colloquially as *Kodala,* and would quip, "Ekach khaay, ani tikde jaay!" (literally meaning, 'Eat this and get lost!') in her unpretentious accent.

Thaalipith is another multigrain flatbread patted and roasted on a tawa. The multigrain mix used for making these fresh breads is called *bhaajni*.

Numerous tiny holes poked in the flatbreads while roasting, allows oil to seep through as they cook. When covered, the steam generated in the tiny spaces allows the bread to remain soft.

Ingredients

Multigrain mix
Sorghum 1 kg

Pearl Millets 1 kg

Rice ½ kg

Wheat 250 g

Moog daal 250 g

Harbaraa daal ½ kg

Pounded rice 100 g

Coriander seeds 200 g

Cumin seeds 100 g

Wash all the grains and dry in the shade.

To make *Thaalipith* you will need
Thaalipith bhaajni 2 cups

Onion 1, finely chopped

Fresh coriander ½ cup finely chopped

Coriander powder 1 tsp

Cumin powder 1 tsp

Turmeric 1 tsp

Red chilli powder 1 tsp

Asafoetida a pinch

Sesame seeds 1 tsp

Carom seeds 1 tsp

Salt to taste

Water to make a very soft dough ¾ cup

For roasting
Oil to roast *Thaalipith* ¼ cup

Method

To make the multigrain mix, set a kadhai on low heat. Gently roast each of the ingredients separately, stirring continuously. This ensures even roasting. Cool and grind the grains into a fine flour. Store in an airtight container. Alternativey, one can mix different flours together e.g. sorghum flour and pearl millet flour in equal quantities, gram flour and rice flour. These flour when dry roasted can be used to make thaalipith.

To make Thaalipith

Mix all the dry ingredients in a bowl. Add chopped onion and chopped coriander leaves and mix, using just enough water make a soft dough. Grease the surface of a cold *tawa* with oil. Divide the dough into four equal portions. Grease your palm with oil. Take a small portion of the dough, place on the greased pan and pat it flat, spreading it evenly on the *tawa* into a disc. Poke small holes in the flatbread. Drizzle a few drops of oil into each hole, cover the pan and place it on medium heat. When the steam generated under the lid makes a sizzling sound, uncover and flip the thalipith to the other side to roast. While one Thaalipith is cooking, pat out another on a second pan, thus saving time. You could also use a sheet of plastic or a silicon sheet to spread the dough and then carefully transfer it to a heated tawa.

Thaalipith goes well with cold yogurt, *loni* or clarified butter and traditional pickles and chutney. These savoury flatbreads tend to vanish almost as soon as they are made!

Tip: Adding vegetables gives these flatbreads a nutritional boost. You can use grated carrots, cucumbers or other vegetables like bottle gourd to make *Thaalipith*. Leftover cooked vegetables or varan are often added the flour and give the Thaalipith an extra crisp texture.

Dhirde

Ingredients

Whole wheat flour 1/2 cup

Sorghum flour 1/2 cup

Gram flour ¼ cup

Rice flour 1 tbs

Coriander powder 1 tsp

Cumin powder 1 tsp

Ginger paste 1 tsp

Garlic paste 1 tsp

Turmeric 1 tsp

Red chilli powder tsp

Asafoetida a pinch

Oil to roast

Salt to taste

Water to make this pancake batter

Method

Mix all the dry ingredients in a bowl. Add the ginger-garlic paste and mix well. Using just enough water, make a batter of pouring consistency. Pour on to a hot pan and spread evenly. Add a few drops of oil along the sides while cooking. Cover and let it cook for a couple of minutes. Flip to the other side and cook until done.

Serve these multigrain *dhirde* (*pancakes*) with chutney or pickle.

Desserts

Babu and Tai

Sadaa-Rangoli-Mangoes

A bit more on Tai's shawl I have mentioned in Pickles section. This was an intricately woven fabric. At times, she would let me use it as a sheet as I napped on our sofa. It was an experience to remember. It definitely was her love that kept me snuggled so warmly. She probably used that beautiful fabric while she cooked on her clay oven in Ambejogai. The fabric was woven with so many of Tai's experiences in her little kitchen.

The moments when she started her day by sprinkling water over the courtyard – a ritual termed *sadaa* that serves to settle the dust on the ground – and making a *rangoli* on the doorstep. Her fingers were tinted a faint red-orange from the vermillion and turmeric she used on her patterns every morning. The sweet smell of the incense she lit after morning puja inside the humble two-room house was trapped in the weave. Wafts of the warm puran poli and the spices she used to lovingly prepare meals for the family found root in the cloth. I would give anything to relive the moments I watched her going through her daily routine.

Babu would walk a long distance to bring us a bounty of *machayche aambe* (Local variety of ripe mangoes usually eaten by softening the fruit and squeezing the pulp manually). My sister and I made sure we wore our oldest frocks and my little brother was made to sit there with just his shorts on! We spent the afternoon on a little platform outside, where a bucket held the tiny mangoes soaking in water. It was an event picking up each mango, pressing it to loosen the fibres and finally to suck out the sweet pulp.

A visit to Tai-Babu was a dual treat for us. Tai often prepared intricate desserts requiring just not patience, but skill and creative flair. She was aware that her grandchildren loved sweets, so she had a stash of goodies in her kitchen stored in large brass *dabbe*. *Ladu, vadya, karanjya*, you name it, it was there. She made sure her kitchen was well organised for us naughty small persons to raid! Best of all, Tai would serve the softest and most delectable *puranachya polya* at mealtime.

The confectionary course does not necessarily conclude a traditional Marathi meal, but could feature as an essential part of the main repast.

Goadache padarth or sweet dishes are all about cooking with water or milk, frying, steaming, pastries filled and fried, sweet fillings in flat breads, desserts sprinkled with sugar or dunked in sugar syrup and much more. Drinks essentially comprise of extracts of naturally occurring fruits that are either mixed with milk or made into a concentrate that lasts months, long enough to get through the harsh summers. A variety of flours is used to create soft puddings like *sheera*, or in making the many kinds of pastry common in this cuisine.

Various auspicious occasions, festivals and rituals are marked by a spread of *goad padaarth*. Festivals are marked by the position of the Sun and the Moon. The food prepared on each occasion is first offered as *naivedya* to the deities, before the meal is shared by the family.

Gudhi padwa is celebrated during Chaitra *shudhh pratipadaa*. The ritual involves hoisting a *gudhi* to mark the start of the Spring season. Puran Poli is generally prepared as *naivedya* for the family deities and the gudhi, though some families offer shrikhand on the day. For Teej Gauri, a delicious pudding of hand-rolled pasta cooked in milk and Karanji filled with jaggery is offered to Gauri, and for Ram Navami, Laadu and Pedha are offered with love to the gods.

Fruits like guavas, mangoes, bananas, gooseberries, kokum and tamarind are used in used in variety of drinks, pickles, as souring agents or even paired with *polya* to make up a quick dessert. Mashed bananas, sugar and warm milk have been a good part of my childhood quick-fix desserts when my fussy young self acted up. Mango pulp extracted from a myriad mango types and a pile of *polya* still steal the show during summer as the most-awaited sweet courses for a true-blue Marathi! There is a ritual of giving a mango to all the ladies during Chaitra Gauri; it is the norm to savour raw mangoes available in the market until this festive occasion.

A variety of *Laadu* is an essential with a *Baalantvida* – a betel nut leaf with a collection of baby clothing is presented by relatives to a new mother on the twelfth day after the birth of a child, or during the naming ceremony. This gift also includes all the nourishment a new mother needs to support her health. Dry fruits, *Aleev Laadu, Methyache Laadu, Dinkaache Laadu*, clarified butter, khobra-lasun chutney, multi-seed mukhwaas and the ingredients required to prepare kheer for the new mother to help strengthen her to nurse her baby.

Khiraapat or Panch Khaadya

Khirapat or Panch Khaadya makes a dry and sweet prasaad especially during Ganesh Chaturthi. It is a mix of 5 different ingredients in different proportions.

Ingredients

Dry coconut grated and dry roasted 1 cup

Dry dates roughly chopped ¼ cup

Poppy seeds roasted 1 tablespoon

Khadi saakhar ¼ cup or powdered sugar ¼ cup

Cardamom powder 1 teaspoon

Method

Dry roast the grated dry coconut in a pan and empty in a bowl. In the same pan, dry roast the poppy seeds and let cool with the coconut. Once dry, mix each of the ingredients mentioned in the list.

Decant into an air-tight container and serve when needed.

. . . .

Phakki or Phanki

This is an interesting quick dessert that is easy to make. Umesh da and Rajesh often recall their childhood, when their *ajji* or *atya* made Phakki.

Ingredients

Whole wheat flour – 1 cup

Tup 1 tsp

Powdered sugar tbsp

Cardamom powder ½ tsp

Method

Roast the whole wheat flour in tup. Roasting in clarified butter gives the four a beautiful fragrant aroma. Mix the fragrant warm flour with powdered sugar and cardamom powder.

Note: You could use grated jaggery instead of powdered sugar for a deeper, treacly flavour. Replace powdered sugar with 2 tablespoons of grated jaggery.

Satyanarayan Pujecha Sheera

This special sheera is traditionally made using a measure of *sawaa* 1.25 for each ingredient. A banana is mashed and mixed in while the sheera is still hot.

Alternatively, you could make sheera using the following proportions:

Ingredients

Rava (semolina) 1 cup

Sugar 3/4 cup

Clarified butter/ghee/tup 3 tbs

Water/ milk approx 1 cup (I like making sheera with milk)

Dry fruits (sliced almonds, halved halved and raisins) to taste

Saffron a pinch.

Cardamom powder a pinch.

Method

Roast the rava with the tup in a heated pan till it releases a lovely aroma and is light gold in colour. Heat the milk/ water and pour it into the roasted semolina. Add crushed saffron and cardomom powder and stir. Cover and cook. When all the liquid is absorbed, lower the heat and stir in the sugar. Cover for a couple of minutes until it is the right consistency. Add the dry fruits, mix well and turn off the heat, leaving the pan covered for a minute or two.

This sheera is best eaten warm.

Gulab Jam

My cousin Anuya recalls her kitchen mishap making Gulab Jam. The fried doughnuts began dissolving in the oil instead of staying intact as round balls. That is when Tai stepped in and eye-balled the dough, and added more flour and mixed it in. She asked Anuya to try frying them once again. "*Ata Krushnacha naav ghe mhanaje sagla neet hoil!*" (recall Lord Krushna's name and all will be well), Tai assured her. Sure enough, each of the balls floated up in the oil, golden brown and in one piece, and Tai grinned. Although she had rectified everything that had gone wrong, she gave all the credit to Lord Krushna.

Ingredients

Khawa (milk solids) 1 cup, grated

Plain flour 2 tbsp

Baking soda 1 pinch (optional)

Sugar 1.5 cups

Water 1.5 cups

Saffron strands a few

Cardamom powder 1 tsp

Oil for frying

Kadhi saakhar (large sugar crystals) 1 handful, to put into the core of the gulab jam

Method

Sugar Syrup

In a pan dissolve the sugar in the water. Heat to boiling – the sugar will form a syrup. Let this simmer for a few minutes and turn the heat off. To this add saffron and cardamom. Set aside.

Dough

Mix together plain flour, baking soda and khawa and knead into a very soft dough. If the dough is too dry, sprinkle in milk. Ideally, a good quality khawa should not require any extra moisture. Pinch off a small amount of dough and flatten it with your palms. Place a couple of khadi saakhar pieces in the centre and fold the dough around the sugar to make small balls. Set these aside. I like adding khadi saakhar – as each ball is fried, the sugar inside melts, keeping the Gulab Jam moist and giving it a special sweet taste in the centre.

Heat oil (or tup, if you prefer) in a pan. Fry the little dough balls till golden brown.

Once fried, drop the balls gently into the sugar syrup and soak them for at least an hour before serving.

Karanji

The pastry and the filling for both Karanji and Modak are the same. Usually the filling for Modak and Karanji comprise of panchkhaadya(mentioned above) made with pithi saakhar in Marathwada. On a few occasions fresh coconut filling is used as a filling.

Ingredients

Pastry/dough

Plain flour 1 cup

Fine semolina ¼ cup

Pinch of salt

Tup 2 tbsp

Milk to knead the dough (about 1/2 cup)

Filling

Fresh coconut 2 cups, grated

Sugar (or jaggery) 1 cup

Nuts (of your choice) 1 tbsp

Roasted poppy seeds 1 tsp

Cardamom powder 1 tsp

Method

For the pastry:

Method

Mix all the ingredients, using milk to knead a semi-soft dough. Cover with a damp cloth for at least 30 mins. Divide into equal portions and shape into balls. Keep covered with a damp cloth.

The filling:

In a pan, mix all the ingredients apart from poppy seeds and cardamom powder. Cook this mixture on a low heat. Stir continuously, making sure the mixture doesn't stick to the bottom of the pan and burn. When the mixture begins to thicken, add the poppy seeds and cook for another couple of minutes. Once done, take the pan off the heat, add cardamom powder and mix well. Let the mixture cool completely.

Assembling:

Roll a ball of dough into a flat circle. Place a small ball of stuffing on the flattened dough and fold the circle to form a semi-circle (karanji). Fold and press the edges of the karanji and pinch closed or use a a fork to press the edges together. Prepare all the karanjis in this way.

Heat oil in a pan to medium hot. Fry the karanji a few at a time till light brown in colour.

Modak

For modak, the dough ball is rolled flat into a circle and the filling placed in the centre. Lift one side of the edge and begin folding into pleats. Continue the pleats around a circle and join in the centre to close the dumpling and make a little 'nose'. Fill the other dough balls in the same way.

As with karanji, fry the modak till light brown in colour.

. . . .

Chirote

Ingredients

Dough

Plain flour 1 cup

Fine semolina ¼ cup

Pinch of salt

Tup 2 tbsp

Milk to knead the dough 1/2 cup

Saatha (Mix for lamination)

Tup 2 tbsp

Rice flour 1 tbsp

Plain flour 1 tbsp

Other Ingredients

Oil or tup for frying

Powdered sugar ½ cup

Method

Whisk the tup until light and fluffy. To this add the two flours a little at a time and keep whisking to mix thoroughly. Set aside.

To make the dough

Mix all the ingredients using a little milk at a time, and knead into a semi-soft dough. Cover with a damp cloth for at least 30 mins. Divide into 4 equal balls.

Roll all the dough balls into flat circles – like *polya* – and set aside under a damp towel. Spread *saatha* evenly on the *poli*. Place another *poli* over it. Spread more saatha evenly over the second *poli*.

135

Roll both the *polya* together like a Swiss roll. Slice this roll into equal parts.

Assemble the other two *polya* in the same way. Once the rolls are cut into pinwheel-like slices, or *chirote*, set them aside on a plate and cover.

Heat oil in a kadhai. While the oil heats up, press each of the slices of layered *polya* (*chirote*) lightly to flatten – use a rolling pin to roll them round and even. Dust with plain flour if needed. Roll all the *chirote* into flat disks.

Fry each *chirote* till crisp and light golden, and drain on a paper towel. Dust powdered sugar generously onto the fried *chirote*.

For *Pakaatle Chirote*, each crisp, flaky chirote is dipped in sugar syrup – similar to that made for Gulab Jam.

. . . .

Shankarpaali

Ingredients

Plain flour 1 cup

Sugar 3 tbsp

Tup 3 tbsp

Milk or water 1/4 cup

Oil for frying

Powdered sugar to dust ¼ cup

Method

Warm the milk, add sugar and dissolve it completely. In a bowl thoroughly mix plain flour and warmed tup; work the tup well into the flour. Add the milk-sugar mix and knead to form a pliable dough. Cover and set aside for half an hour.

Roll the dough flat And using a *kaatan* or pizza cutter, cut it into small diamond shapes.

Heat oil in a deep frying pan and lower the heat to medium. Fry the diamond-shaped Shankarpali till they are golden brown and crisp. Drain on a kitchen towel and sprinkle with powdered sugar. Store in an air-tight container.

Naaralachya Laadu / Vadyaa

Trupti, my sister-in-law, and Saroja *atya* make the best *laadu* I know of. I guess they have their mother's genes. Trupti's makes the best *Taalula chikatnaara* (which sticks to the palate as you eat) besanacha laadu.

Ingredients

1 coconut scraped

Milk 1 cup

Sugar 1 cup

Cardamom powder 1 tsp (I like adding rose extract)

Slivers of blanched almonds

Rose petals (optional)

Tup for greasing

Method

Into a thick bottomed pan on medium heat add all the ingredients apart from the tup. Mix well and stir continuously. When the mixture begins to thicken and leave the sides of the pan, add cardamom powder or rose extract. Once the mixture is thick enough but still easy to spread, turn off the heat.

Pour the mixture out on to a greased surface. Spread it flat and garnish with almond slivers and rose petals. Roll it flat and even with a greased rolling pin. Cut into squares or diamonds, or roll into small balls like laadu.

Store in an air-tight container.

Besanaache Ladu

Ingredients

Besan (gram flour) 1 cup

Semolina 1 tbsp (optional, it adds a texture to the laadu and avoids sticking to the palate if one doesn't wish)

Tup ¼ cup

Powdered sugar ¾ cup

Cardamom powder 1 tsp

Raisins or cashews fried in tup

Method

In a pan, melt a little tup. Roast semolina until it turns slightly pink and gives off a nutty aroma. Set this aside. To the rest of the tup, add gram flour and roast. The mixture loosens slightly at first and then, once it begins cooking, it thickens gradually. Add this to the roasted semolina. Cool the mixture slightly, add cardamom, chopped nuts and powdered sugar. Mix well and roll into small spheres.

Note: Rolling Marathwadi laadu *valne*, differs slightly because the spheres have flat top and base just like a pedha.

· ·

Gul Paadpdi

Ingredients

Wheat flour 1 cup

Jaggery 1/2 cup, grated

Tup ¼ cup

Cardamom powder 1 tsp

Nuts of a your choice a handful

Method

In a pan, melt the ghee and roast the whole wheat flour. Once the flour gains a nice colour and aroma, add jaggery and mix well. Add the cardamom powder and stir to mix thoroughly. Pour into a pre-greased plate and smooth level. If you wish, garnish with chopped nuts. Cut into bite-sized squares. This measure makes 10 squares.

Instead of making squares, one can also roll them into *laadu* spheres.

Dind

Shraavan rings in a string of religious occasions. Each holds a unique significance. Each festival demands a special meal too. And every household has a special way of celebrating. *Naag Panchami* is celebrated with a lot of vigour, especially by the women. They adorn their palms with beautiful henna patterns and wear colourful attire. It is the first *Panchami* in the Hindu calendar and they enjoy being outdoors and playing on swings. The women of the house pre-plan meals, making sure that no chopping or frying is done in the kitchen on the auspicious day. They pay obeisance to *Naag Devta* (Snake God).

Our family meal comprises of vegetables chopped a day in advance and steamed Dind, sometimes referred to as *kadbu*.

Ingredients

Wheat flour 3 cups

Salt 1 tsp

Turmeric 1 tsp

Oil/tup 2 tbs plus some more to make the dough smooth

Knead the dough and set aside.

Rice powder/wheat flour 1 cup to roll the *polis*

Filling

Harbaraa daal 3 cups, washed and pressure cooked

Jaggery 1.5 cups, grated

Nutmeg powder 1/2 tsp

Cardamom powder 1/2 tsp

Few strands of saffron

Dough

Prepare a pliable dough using the following ingredients. Set aside.

Wheat flour 3 cups

Salt 1/2 tsp

Turmeric 1/2 tsp

Oil/ghee 1 tbs to make the dough smooth

Method

Pressure cook the dal until soft, then drain it in a sieve. Save the stock separately for Kataachi Amti. Once all the stock is retrieved from the cooked daal, the daal should be cool and dry, but soft – it should mash when you press it between your fingers. If it still seems moist, spread it out on paper towels to remove any liquid. Transfer the dry daal into a heavy pan. Add jaggery and cook

139

the mixture on medium heat, stirring continuously. Some people like adding sugar to the mixture, but I prefer my filling with jaggery and I like it soft. The mixture will soften and become a reddish brown colour. When it is done, the daal and jaggery will be completely mixed and the mixture will come together, leaving the sides of the pan. Add the cardamom powder, saffron and nutmeg powder and mix well. Turn the heat off and set aside to cool.

Prepare a steamer or idli pan – pour in the water to heat and grease the steamer container. Roll out the prepared flour dough and place some filling in the centre. Bring the edges together, so that the puran is completely enclosed in the dough. My mother-in-law trained me in folding the ends of *kadbu*. These could easily be sealed using *kaatan* (similar to pizza cutters) to cut the extra pastry off. However, she preferred folding or crimping the edges – referred to as *murad* – intricately, giving them a beautiful and effective seal.

Place the kadbu/Dinds in the steamer. Steam for 10 mins. Serve piping hot with a dollop of ghee and Purnachi Aamti.

Naachni Laadu

Simple resources like *naachni* (finger millet), tup, jaggery, flattened rice, nuts and cardamom are packed into these Ladus. They are very quick to make and are great for breakfast. You could use sugar instead of jaggery for sweetness.

Ingredients

Naachni 4 cups (or use half-half mix of whole wheat flour and naachni)

Jaggery 2.5 cups, grated (you can add or decrease for to taste)

Clarified butter 1/2 cup

Cardamom 4-5 pods, deseeded and the seeds crushed

Pounded or flattened rice(medium) 1 handful

Nuts of your choice chopped

Method

Melt the tup in a pan. Fry the flattened rice in the tup. Drain and place in a bowl into which you will add the roasted Laadu mix. When cooled, crush the fried flattened rice with your palms. In the same hot ghee, roast the naachni until it has a sweet aroma. Add this to the fried flattened rice. Cool the mixture slightly, then add cardamom, chopped nuts and grated jaggery. Mix well and roll into small spheres.

The same method can be used to make whole wheat flour ladus.

Boondiche Laadu

Ingredients

For the Boondi

Gram flour 2 cups

Water 1 cup

Tup/oil 1 tablespoon

Oil for frying

Dry fruits to taste,
Powdered

For the Syrup

Sugar 2 cups

Water 1.5 cups

Saffron a pinch

Cardamom powder 1tsp

Method

For making the syrup, place all the ingredients in a pan and bring to a boil. Reduce the heat and simmer until the syrup is of ½ thread consistency. Keep testing the syrup to check its consistency. To do this, dip a wooden spatula in the mixture and lift it out. When it is cool enough, dip your clean and dry forefinger into the syrup and then touch that finger to your thumb and pull apart gently.

Half-thread consistency is reached when a single thread is formed and breaks immediately when your forefinger and your thumb are pulled apart gently. Switch off the gas and set the pan aside.

For making the mix water into gram flour, a little at a time to avoid lumps. Add ghee or oil – this will improve the consistency and crunch. Add the food colouring or saffron (soaked in a little of the water measured out for the batter). Heat oil in a deep pan. Using a perforated ladle, drop small rounds of batter through the holes into the oil. Pushing gently with a spoon makes for better boondi. Once cooked, drain the boondi and put directly into the syrup. Let the boondi soak well in the syrup. The orange colour of the boondi and the saffron in the syrups together give the Laadu a lovely colour.

Once the boondi is well soaked, add in the ground dry fruits and mix. Rub your palms with a little oil/tup and shape the sweetened gem-like boondi into balls. This needs some patience but the result is well worth it. You should have 25 little jewels to relish.

Tilache Laadu

Ingredients

White sesame seeds 1 cup

Jaggery/gud 1 cup

Peanuts 1/2 cup, roasted and powdered

Tup 1/4 cup

Cardamom powder 1/2 tsp

Method

Roast the sesame seeds. Dry grind to a powder. Heat the ghee in a pan and add the jaggery. The jaggery will melt and start to foam. Take the pan off the heat and add the sesame seeds, ground peanuts and cardamom powder. Mix well. Roll the mixture into small laadu or smooth flat into a greased tray and cut into squares while still warm using a wet knife.

. . . .

Udidache Laadu

Ingredients

Udid daal 1 cup, roasted and ground coarsely

Clarified butter ½ cup

Sugar ½ cup

Milk to drizzle on the roasted flour (2 tbs)

Cardamom powder 1 tsp

Chopped nuts and raisins

Method

In a pan, melt the tup and add the Udid daal powder. Roast until the daal gives off a sweet aroma. Over this, sprinkle milk, cover and set aside. This allows the roasted particles to fluff up. While the mix is still warm, add sugar, nuts, raisins and cardamom powder and roll into small balls.

Moog daal laadu can be made in a similar way.

Dinkaache Laadu

Ingredients

Khobra grated ¾ cup

Badam ground coarsely ¾ cup

Kharik powder ¾ cup

Khuskhus ½ tbsp

Manuka ½ cup

Dink 2/3 cup

Wilaychi ½ tsp

Tup 1.5 cups

Kanik 1.5 cups

Gul 2 cups grated

Method

In a pan, dry roast khobra till lightly brown and set aside. Dry roast poppy seeds as well and set aside.

Heat a couple of tablespoon of tup. Turn the heat down and add dink to it. Fry till the edible gum plumps up and when you press it should crumble and feel sticky inside.

Grind roasted coconut, poppy seeds and the fried edible gum together.

In the rest of the tup, roast the whole wheat flour till it exudes a lovely aroma, is slightly pink in colour and feels light.

To the roasted flour, add the coarsely ground almonds, dried dates powder, raisins, edible gum-coconut-poppy seeds mix and grated jaggery. Mix well so that jaggery begins to melt in the hot mixture. Turn the heat off. Add the cardamom powder and mix well. Roll into spheres while the mixture is still warm.

Note: You can add *Jayphal*(Nutmeg) grated ½ tsp for flavouring as well.

One may even add ¼ cup of *Godambi* ground coarsely to this and Fenugreek seeds ground fine ¼ cup to make a very nutritious laadu which is often prescribed for new mothers or people suffering from back pain.

Maidyache Laadu

Ingredients

Plain flour 3 cups

Semolina 1 cup

Tup 1.5 cups

Powdered sugar 1.5 cups

Cardamom powder tsp

Method

In a pan melt half a cup of tup. Roast semolina in the melted tup until it turns slightly pink and gives off a delicious aroma. Set this aside. To the rest of the tup, add plain flour and roast till the mixture turns light pink. Add this to the bowl of roasted semolina. Cool the mixture slightly, add cardamom, chopped nuts and powdered sugar. Mix well and roll into small spheres.

Rawaa Laadu

Ingredients

Fine semolina 1 cup

Sugar 3/4 cup

Tup ½ cup

Cardamom powder 1 tsp

Raisins a handful

Method

Mix the rawa with the tup and set aside for 5-6 hours. Break up any lumps and roast until pink in colour and fragrant. Cool and grind to get a finer grain. Add powdered sugar and cardamom powder and mix well mix. Roll into small balls and press a raisin on top of each to garnish.

Note: A portion of *Ravyaachi Kheer* is often served to a new mother every morning to fulfil her nutritional requirements. This can be made by roasting semolina in butter clarified as mentioned above. Then it is cooked in 2 cups of milk for 3-4 mins and sugar is added to taste. After stirring and cooking this mixture until it thickens, the heat is turned off. A flavouring of cardamom and a few roasted cashewnuts completes this delicious dessert.

Aalivaache Laadu

Ingredients

Aleev 1/2 cup

Tup 2 tbs

Fresh coconut 1.5 cups grated

Gul 1.5 cups grated

Coconut water 1cup

Method

Soak *aleev* in coconut water for a couple of hours. This helps the seeds to plump up. Place a thick bottom pan on heat, add grated coconut and *gul* and mix well. Turn the heat down and cook for a couple of minutes till *gul* dissolves. To this add soaked *aleev* and cook the mixture on slow heat, stirring continuously. Heat a couple of tablespoon of *tup* and cook the mixture until it leaves the sides of the pan. Turn the heat off. Roll into spheres while the mixture is still warm.

Anaarse

Sudha *atya* makes the most decadent anaarse. The main element is getting the rice flour right. Anyone making anaarse needs to make sure the soaked and dried rice is pounded well which is done manually in the *khal batta* into a fine flour by the pros in our kitchen. Thus one needs to appreciate the patience and the time involved in making Anaarse. Initially, I was also apprehensive about making the sweet treat the traditional way, from scratch. But as our *aais* and *aajjis* always said, patience is a virtue – three days of soaking, and drying the rice just enough, making sure not to over-dry it, or else *tukda padto,* that is: the Anaarse break. Then making the dough with jaggery! I even tried frying them instantly – they started disintegrating, a state colloquially termed *anaarse hasle*, or the anaarse laughed! But once I made it a point to put the container away for three or four days, away from my eye-sight to avoid the urge to check on them, they worked.

Ingredients

Ambemohor rice 1 cup

Jaggery grated 1 cup

Poppy seeds to garnish ¼ cup

Ghee to fry

Method

Soak the rice for 3 days and change the water every day. On the 4th day, drain out all the water. Spread the rice on a kitchen towel in a shade and let dry for a couple of hours. Grind the rice into a fine flour. Sieve to get a finer flour. To the flour add an equal quantity of jaggery and rub in slowly to make a soft dough. You may need to add a spoon of milk to help the dough along. But that is a last resort. Place the dough in an air-tight container and forget about it for about 4 days!

This dough can be placed in the fridge to be used on the day you want to make anaarse. To fry the anaarse, heat clarified butter in a pan. Grease your palm and roll the dough into small balls. Flatten each and top with poppy seeds. Deep fry until crisp. The anaarse develop a beautiful mesh once they are fried.

Shrikhand

Traditionally, Shrikhand is made using *chakka*, or hung curd. *Chakka* is made by hanging yoghurt in muslin and letting it drain overnight. As a child, I remember Aai making Shrikhand with *chakka* (she hung the muslin bundle on a tap with a *paraat* or a plate with a wide rim underneath). The whey which drained out of the *chakka* was used to make chapatti dough. During our stay in Kolkata, when she had no *puran yantra* (food mill) to mix the *chakka* and sugar thoroughly, Aai would use a *sapeethachi chalni* (a sieve) with a fine mesh. It was fun, sitting on the floor to help Aai – she would hand over a *fulpatra* (steel tumbler) or a *vaati* (a small bowl) to press the *chakka* and sugar mix on the sieve to pass through it. Once she got enough of the silky, sweet-sour blend, Aai would mix in a couple of tablespoons of milk infused with saffron and stir in cardamom crushed on her *polpaat* (a circular board for rolling polya). Finally came the chopped nuts (almonds, pistachios, etc), folded into the mix as a garnish. The hard work paid off when we got the creamiest Shrikhand to eat.

Ingredients

Chakka 2 cups

Sugar 1.5 cups

Chopped nuts

Saffron strands infused in warm milk

Cardamom powder

Method

Place the puran yantra, food mill on a pot or vessel it fits. Mix a small portion of yogurt with sugar. Pass it through the food mill. Carry on mixing sugar through the food mill with the rest of the yogurt. Add saffron infused milk and cardamom powder. Garnish with nuts of your choice.

Dudhi Halwa

Ingredients

Bottle gourd 2 cups, grated

Milk 1.5 cups

Sugar 1/2 cup

Tup 1 tbsp for frying the dry fruits

2 tbsp to cook the halwa

Khawa 1/4 cup

Chopped nuts (cashews, almonds) and raisins 7-8

Method

Almonds: soak them in water for a couple of hours and peel off the skin. Chop the nuts into thin slivers.

Cashews: fry them in tup until light brown and set aside.

Raisins: Fry these in tup and set aside

Melt the tup in a thick-bottomed pan. Add the grated dudhi and mix continuously until the water has evaporated. Add milk and boil, then reduce the heat to simmer, stirring all the while. The dudhi will soften gradually and when the milk is reduced to less than half the original quantity , add sugar and mix well. Add grated khawa to give a rich and creamy texture to the halwa. Cook for another 2-3 minutes. Garnish with chopped nuts and raisins.

Gaajaracha Halwa

Ingredients

Grated carrots 2 cups

Tup 2 tbsp

Milk 2 cups

Cardamom powder 1 tsp

Sugar 1/4 cup

Raisins a few, fried in tup

Chopped nuts (cashews, almonds) 7-8, slivered and fried in a tbsptup

Method

Melt tup in a thick-bottomed pan. Add the grated carrots and mix well on a low heat. Add milk and stir continuously. Bring to a boil and then reduce to a simmer. The carrots will cook and soften gradually. The milk will be reduced to less than half by this time. Add sugar and mix well. Cook for another 2-3 minutes. Garnish with chopped nuts and raisins.

. . . .

Masala Doodh

Milk flavoured with this nutty and aromatic masala is devoured on the evening of Kojagiri Pournima when the community enjoys a late night picnic either on the house terrace or in the garden, sipping cups of masala doodh.

Ingredients

Charoli (*Buchanania lanzan*), pistachios, cashews, almonds ½ cup, ground coarsely

Cardamom powder 1 tsp

Nutmeg powder 1/8 tsp

Saffron strands ¼ tsp

Method

Mix these ingredients to make *doodh masala*.

Pour 4 cups of milk into a pan. Add 4 tbsp of sugar. Simmer until sugar dissolves. Bring to a boil and add 2 tbsp of doodh masala and stir. Pour hot into cups and serve.

Shevayanchi Kheer

Ingredients

Shevaya ¼ cup

Milk 3 cups

Sugar 1/2 cup

Tup 1 tsp to fry dry fruits

Tup 1 tbsp to roast shevai

Cardamom powder ½ tsp

Chopped nuts (cashews, almonds) and raisins

Water ½ cup

Method

Peel the almonds and sliver. Chop the cashews and fry in tup until golden brown and set aside.

Heat a pan to medium. Pour in tup and add shevaya. Roast the shevaya until light brown. Turn off the heat and add water. Strain the shevaya through a sieve to drain out the water. Doing this helps get rid of the salt which is often added when making vermicelli and can split the milk when cooking kheer.

Into a thick-bottomed pan, pour milk and stir gently on medium heat. Add the roasted and drained shevaya. Simmer, stirring continuously, till the milk reduces to half. Add sugar. Cook for another few minutes. Add cardamom powder and garnish with chopped nuts.

Khapli Gavhachi Kheer

Khapli gahu or Emmer wheat is very fibrous and thus has therapeutic properties. This kheer is made with jaggery giving it a lovely, rich and decadent treacly taste.

Ingredients

Khapli gahu 1 cup, soaked for a 6-7 hours, ideally overnight

Milk 1 cup

Jaggery grated 1/2 cup

Tup 1 tbsp

Cardamom ½ tsp

Chopped nuts (cashews, almonds) and raisins 7-8, peeled, cut, fried in tup

Water approximately 2 cups to pressure cook

Method

Pressure cook the soaked *khapli gahu* for 6 whistles on medium heat. Reduce the heat to low and cook for 5 minutes. Drain the water into another pan and use for cooking dal, making kadhi or even kneading dough for *polya*. Grind the cooked wheat coarsely in a blender.

In a thick-bottomed pan, add tup and coarsely ground *gahu*. Stir for a few minutes until mixed well. To this add grated jaggery and stir to incorporate. Cook for another 5 minutes and turn the heat off. Add lukewarm milk gradually to avoid curdling. Place the pan back on the heat and cook for another couple of minutes. Add cardamom powder and garnish with nuts and raisins.

Panha

Ingredients

Raw Mangoes (medium size) 2

Sugar or jaggery 3 tbsp

Salt a pinch

Saffron 5-6 strands

Cardamom seeds crushed 1/2 tsp

Method

Wash the mangoes. Traditionally raw mangoes are boiled until they are soft. Alternatively, you may pressure cook them to save time. My mother roasts the mangoes. Fire roasted mango gives this drink a lovely smoky, barbeque-like taste.

Prick the mangoes as you would to brinjal before roasting. I would advise you to cover the sides of the cooktop with foil or roast the fruit in a paapad roaster like I have done, to avoid the juices spoiling your workplace. Roast the mangoes till they feel soft and smell cooked.

Once the mangoes are cooked by either of the methods mentioned above, peel off the skin, scoop the cooked pulp off the seed and mash well. Blend the pulp with a cup of water. Mix sugar or jaggery if you are using it. Add water to adjust the consistency. Add salt and crushed cardamom.

Note: Cumin freshly roasted and crushed and added to the juice gives it a great taste.

Limbache Sarbat

Summer holidays at Aajji-Dada's home were fun, because there was food and drink for every part of the day. Each morning 5-6 lemons were placed in a *paraat* or a *bhaanda* (kitchen vessel) under a large *maath* (clay pot) placed close to the back door so that it would be well ventilated. These clay pots held drinking water. As the water within seeped out through the clay, it evaporated, thus cooling the surface of the pot and eventually the water it held. A wet *pancha* (cloth) was always wrapped around the clay pot to keep it cooler. Sometimes water dripped from the bottom of these clay pots. A flat pan was placed to catch these cold drips. Lemons kept in this water cooled down naturally. This was the norm before refrigerators were a common utility. Come 4 pm, the ladies of the house would beckon us children for snacks and a glass of Limbache Sarbat.

Ingredients	Method
Juice of 6 lemons	Squeeze the lemons to extract the juice. Get rid of the seeds. Add sugar and salt; stir to dissolve.
Sugar 1 cup	
Salt 1 tsp	
Cardamom powder	Sieve and pour in an air-tight jar. Store in the fridge.
Saffron strands	
Water	To serve, dilute the extract with water. Add cardamom powder and saffron.

Kavathache Sarbat

Ingredients

Kavath/ Wood apple 1

Gul/ Jaggery ½ cup

Water

Method

Extract the pulp from the fruit. Deseed the pulp and mix with jaggery. Add water to taste to make this simplest and cooling drink.

. . . .

Amsulache Sarbat

I recall Smita *mavshi* bringing home fresh, deep red kokum fruits, *Garcinia indica* (belonging to the mangosteen family). She would chop the fruit and discard the pulp; saving the skins shaped like cups. She would set aside a jar to soak these fresh skins in sugar. After setting the jar aside in the sun, the sugar and the kokum together made the best syrup. Most of my afternoons were spent staring at the jar, with the sugar dissolving into a gorgeous carmine liquid. The *agal* (syrup) was drained into a separate jar to be used to serve the family and guests with a cooling drink during the grimy summers.

Ingredients

Kokum *agal* 4 tablespoons

Cumin powder ½ tsp

Salt ¼ tsp

Water.

Sugar 2 tsp if required

Method

Stir *agal* with salt and cumin powder in a jug. Add more sugar if required. Pour into a tall glass to serve.

Doodh Halad

Ingredients

Milk 2 cups

Turmeric 1 tsp

Sugar or jaggery 1 tbsp

Method

Mix all the ingredients together in a pan. Simmer till the sugar dissolves and then boil. You could add saffron to the preparation for extra richness. Warm cup of doodh halad helps beat the cold and cough.

. . . .

Gavti Chahaa Ghalun Chahaa

Ingredients

Water 2 cups

Milk 1 cup (add or reduce the quantity of milk to taste)

Sugar 2 tsp

Tea leaves 2 tsp

Lemongrass two twigs

Ginger 1 tsp (optional)

Cardamom powder 1/2 tsp (optional)

Method

In a saucepan, mix water, lemongrass, ginger, cardamom powder and sugar. Bring to a boil. Add tea leaves and simmer for a minute. Turn the heat off and cover for a couple of minutes. Pour in warm milk and turn the heat back on. Bring to a quick boil and strain into teacups.

All about Fasting

With Panji and Shruti

A Morsel

Any Marathi child will vouch for Sabudana Khichadi as a favourite. As a little girl I recall waiting for Aai's *upaas* (fast) so that I could feast on this light food. Just a *ghaas* (morsel, usually a mouthful) from her plate would make me happy. When I moved to Pune for further studies, I would make an effort to travel all the way from Kothrud to Hadapsar to visit Sangeeta *mavshi* on Thursdays to grab my share of *Saabudaana Khichadi*.

Many people practice fasting as a religious observance. Fasting on a particular day signifies paying obeisance to the deity. Abstaining from regular food and relishing tubers like potatoes and sweet potatoes, fruits, samo (barnyard millet) and sago seeds during religious occasions, especially during certain months, is an age-old practice.

Weather conditions especially during the monsoon are not favourable to digest a multicourse meal. Intermittent fasting and eating light food in these conditions helps the body endure adverse climates. For those who do physical labour, high starch content food like sago, samo and tubers provides energy required by the body for day-to-day activities.

Thus Sabudaanaa khichadi, bhagar, thalipith made with upaasaachi bhaajani are mainly prefered food to eat when fasting. Peanuts laadu made in jaggery or even steamed sweet potatoes in jaggery and tup are relished as desserts during fasting along with fresh seasonal fruits. Upaasaachi Bhaajni is prepared by roasting Samo seeds, amaranth seeds and sago seeds mixed in the ratio 1:1:1/2. The fine flour prepared by grinding these seeds makes a quintessential *Upaasaachi Bhaajani*. This *bhajani* is flavoured with roasted cumin powder. Upasaache thaalipith are patted by mixing boiled potatoes which serve the purpose of binding too.

Daanyachi Aamti

Ingredients

Peanuts 1 cup, roasted, crushed

Water 2 cups

Amsul 4-5, soaked in quarter cup of water

Green chillies 2

Cumin seeds 2 tsp

Method

Grind green chillies, amsul, salt, sugar and 1 tsp of cumin seeds. To this add crushed peanuts and ½ cup water and grind well.

In a pan heat tup. To this add cumin seeds and let splutter. To this add the peanuts mixture. Add rest of the water and cook on low heat. Keep stirring until this aamti simmers.

Serve with sabudana khichadi or with bhagar.

....

Sabudana Vada

Ingredients

Sago seeds 2 cups, washed and soaked for 5-6 hours or overnight

Potato 1, boiled and grated

Peanuts 3/4 cup, roasted, crushed

Green chillies, 2, crushed

Sugar ¼ tsp

Salt

Oil for frying

Method

In a bowl mix soaked sago seeds, green chillies, potato, crushed peanuts, salt and sugar. Potato helps bind the mixture. Make small balls and press to flatten slightly.

Heat oil in a deep frying pan. On low heat, fry each of the *vada* until golden brown. Drain on a kitchen towel.

Serve with yogurt.

Upasachi Bataatyachi Bhaaji

This potato side is made without adding turmeric and the usual spice blend. Instead it is flavoured with clarified butter and cumin seeds.

Ingredients

Boiled potatoes, chopped into pieces 4

Green chillies 2

Cumin seeds 2 tsps

Roasted, crushed peanuts 2 tbss

Salt to taste

Sugar 1 tsp

Tup 1 tbs

Method

In a bowl, mix chopped potatoes, salt, sugar and crushed peanuts.

Heat *tup* in a pan. Add cumin seeds and green chillies. Add potatoes and coat well with the tempering. Mix well on low heat to avoid the potatoes burning. Cover and cook for 3-4 minutes. Squeeze in lemon. Serve with *Sabudana Khichadi* or *Bhagar* and chilled yogurt.

....

Rataalyache Kaap

Ingredients

Sweet potatoes 2, cut in roundels

Clarified butter 1 tbs

Jaggery 1.5 tbs

Water 1/4 cup

Method

In a pan dissolve jaggery in water and bring to a boil.

In another pan heat *tup*. To this add the sweet potato roundels and sauté until soft.

Place the fried sweet potatoes in the jaggery syrup.

You may add sautéed nuts to the potatoes.

Sabudana Khichadi

Ingredients

Sago seeds 2 cups, washed and soaked for 5-6 hours or overnight

Potato 1, boiled and chopped

Tup 1 tbs

Cumin seeds ½ tsp

Peanuts 3/4 cup, roasted, crushed

Green chillies 2, chopped

Sugar ¼ tsp

Salt to taste

Lemon juice

Method

In a bowl, mix soaked sago seeds, crushed peanuts, salt and sugar.

Heat *tup* in a pan. Add cumin seeds and green chillies. Add potatoes and coat well with the tempering. Add sago. Mix well and cover. Turn the heat to low to avoid burning. Uncover and mix occasionally for even cooking. Cover and cook for another 5 minutes until all the sago is translucent. Squeeze in lemon juice and serve with chilled yogurt.

Many families in Marathwada make *Sabudana Khichadi* with red chilli powder instead of green chillies – *Lal rangachi sabudana khichadi* (red coloured sabudana khichadi) is a favourite with many children in our family. Pratibha *atya* makes it that way.

Soaked sabudana, salt, roasted and crushed peanuts, boiled potatoes are mixed and patted into thalipith discs at other times.

Bhagar

This is a soft gruel of samo seeds which is cooked in clarified butter and seasoned. Crushed peanuts add texture to the preparation. A squeeze of lime juice finishes it to a perfect fasting meal.

Ingredients

Samo seeds 1 cup

Tup 1 tbs

Cumin seeds ½ tsp

Peanuts ½ cup, roasted, crushed

Green chillies 2, chopped

Sugar ¼ tsp

Salt

Water 1 cup

Lemon juice

Method

Roast samo seeds in a pan on low heat until a nice aroma is released. Set aside. Heat *tup* in a pan. Add cumin seeds and green chillies and sauté briefly. Pour water into this and boil. Add the samo seeds. Mix well and cover. Turn the heat to low until the seeds are cooked. Squeeze in lemon juice and serve with chilled yogurt.

Bataatyache Kees

Ingredients

Potatoes 2, grated and placed in water

Tup 2 tbs

Cumin seeds 1 tsp

Peanuts ½ cup, roasted, crushed

Green chillies 2, chopped

Sugar ¼ tsp

Salt

Water 1 cup

Grated fresh coconut

Lemon

Method

Heat *tup* in a pan. Add cumin seeds and green chillies and sauté for a couple of minutes. Squeeze water out of the grated potatoes and add to the tempering. Mix well and cover. Turn the heat to low until the potatoes soften slightly. Add salt, sugar and crushed peanuts and mix well. Cover and cook for another 3-4 minutes.

Squeeze in lemon juice, garnish with grated fresh coconut and serve with chilled yogurt.

Rajgira Kheer

Ingredients

Rajgira (amaranth seeds) 1 cup

Jaggery 1/2 cup

Milk 2 cups

Cardamom powder 1 tsp

Soaked almonds, peeled and chopped to garnish (optional)

Saffron few strands to garnish

Method

Pressure cook rajgira with half a cup of water by tying in a musin. Once done, add milk and let the mix boil for some time. Add the jaggery and cardamom powder. Garnish with chopped almonds and saffron. Serve hot or cold.

Traditional Hand-Rolled Pasta

Shobhana Patki and Late Ujjwala Deo

Hand-rolled pasta: Marathwadi food is mainly country fare, with a combination of textures, techniques and tastes of various kinds covering all the nutrient categories. Often a meal will include pasta of one kind or another. It may be served as a steamed, boiled or fried side to add texture to the spread that is on offer, or as part of a great pudding – kheer is made using the vermicelli commonly referred to as *shevaya*. Fresh pasta could also go into a one-pot meal when the family wants a quick meal.

Hand-rolled or hand pressed pasta in Marathi cuisine can be, broadly divided into dry and fresh varieties.

Hand-rolled or hand pressed pasta in Marathi cuisine can be, broadly divided into dry like *Gavhale, Shevaya, Kurdaya* and fresh varieties like *Ukad Shengule* and *Varan Phala*.

I have shared savoury recipes using the pasta varieties in this chapter. The sweet variations can be found in the chapter exploring "Desserts".

Valvat, Gavhale

My earliest memory of hand-rolled pasta is of Yermalkar *ajji*, my maternal grandmother, rolling them with her dextrous hands at her sister's house. The family had gathered to gear up for a wedding. The house was full of people bustling around. While the young ladies cleared up the kitchen after lunch, the clan of aunts sat beside the elderly ladies in the next room. The menfolk had either decided to catch up with chores outside or find a place to recline in the bedroom until afternoon tea. I was one among the group of children happily dashing through the rooms. The giggles in the kitchen were as audible as the elderly ladies moaning about the next female generation being slow coaches and how quick and organised they were in their times. Ajji and her sister groaned at the leisurely pace of the ladies in the kitchen and asked them to hurry up and join them. It all suggested that we had a busy afternoon ahead of us.

Very soon, all the ladies gathered around a paat (a low levelled table) and a paraat (shallow bottom vessel used for kneading) that held a dough. Each lady picked up a handful of tools, including a comb, a wooden stick and a few other pieces. I sat next to my mother, watching each distinct shape emerging. The dextrous fingers of the ladies rolled and twisted the dough as the elder generation kept vigil to make sure of the size and shape of the unique variations being made.

A gathering like this usually has a traditional song sung by both the young and the old, a casual gossip, chitchat and occasional teasing of the bride-to-be. I call this a subtle way of holding a 'hen do' in the family, since the would-be bride or groom is traditionally not allowed to go out for about a week before D-day. By tea time, the ladies had assortments of hand rolled and twisted pasta called valvat or gavhale ready, set out on plates to dry.

The pasta are shaped intricately to resemble rice grains, pearls, rings, shells or even teardrops. Some may be twisted to add interest. Each shape has a name, for example *maltya, chighor, pohe, phule, fanolya* (made using a *phani*/comb), *mohol, nakhavlya* and more. *Gavhale* or *valvat* are often offered to the groom prior to the wedding, just before he visits the temple to pay obeisance to Lord *Maruti*. The same hand rolled valvat is served in *Vihinichi Pangat*, when the wedding ritual culminates. The bride's family has the honour of serving five variations in kheer to the groom's family. Valvat is lightly fried in clarified butter (tup) and cooked with milk and sugar to make a dessert for the guests.

The main ingredients of the pasta are whole wheat or plain flour and semolina, in the ratio of 4:1. Milk is used to bind the dough. The dough sits for a few hours and then is ready to be used. Ideally, the ladies prepare the dough early in the morning; by the time the household has lunch, the dough is ready to be pounded in the *khal-batta* to work up the gluten and be made ready to roll into various shapes. Deo Aai preferred making valvat using semolina alone.

Ukad Shengule

Ukad Shengule is a favourite one-pot meal. My son, Pranav, loves the taste of freshly made flour pasta in tempered stock, sometimes flavoured with buttermilk, which gives it a distinctive dimension. The sour buttermilk paired with the spices results in a riot of flavours in every mouthful! A simple and quick dish to make and equally easy to digest.

Ingredients

For the Shengule

Sorghum flour 1 cup
Whole wheat flour 1/2 cup
Gram flour 1/4 cup
Garlic 2-3 cloves
Green chillies 2
Salt

Turmeric 1 tsp
Red chilli powder 1 tsp
Asafoetida a pinch
Carom seeds 1 tsp

For the tempering

Oil 1 tbsp
Cumin ½ tsp
Mustard seeds 1/2 tsp

Curry leaves 9-10
Turmeric 1tsp
Red chilli powder 1tsp
Asafoetida a pinch
Salt to taste
Water 2.5 cups
Buttermilk 1 cup (optional)
Coriander finely chopped, to garnish

Method

Mix all the dry ingredients. Crush garlic and green chillies together with a little salt. Add this to the dry mix and form into a dough with water, firm enough to roll into shapes. Divide the dough into portions. Roll each portion into a thin, long sausage. Cut each sausage into smaller pieces and form them into loops. Leave a small piece of dough aside to thicken the soup later.

In a pan heat oil and temper with cumin seeds and mustard seeds. Add curry leaves, turmeric, red chilli powder and asafoetida, and pour in 2.5 cups of water. Bring this to a boil.

Add the loops to the boiling water and spices. Dissolve the reserved dough in buttermilk, if using or use water. Add this mix to the boiling water, loops pasta and spices. Stir well. Very soon the mixture will begin thickening. Cover and cook for 10 minutes. Once the loops are cooked, turn off the heat. Garnish with chopped coriander.

A bowl of piping hot Ukad Shengule goes well with garlic-sesame Bhurka.

Note: You may add a vegetable puree (e.g. spinach puree) to the flour mix for both colour and nutritional value.

. . . .

Pithlyachya Vadyanchi Aamti

When *Pithle, Shengule* and *Zunka* seem easy and quick meal options, *Pithlyachya Vadyanchi Aamti* joins the quick meal list.

Ingredients

Gram flour 1 cup

Salt ½ tsp

Coriander chopped ¼ cup

For the tempering

Oil 2 tsp

Mustard seeds 1 tsp

Asafoetida a pinch

Curry leaves 8-10

Coriander, chopped

Water 1 cup

Salt for seasoning (use a tad bit less, because savoury vadya will be added to seasoned aamti)

For the Aamti

Harbaraa dal 1/4 cup

Red chilli powder 1 tsp

Turmeric 1 tsp

Onion ½, chopped

Roasted coconut 2 tbs

Coriander, chopped

Ginger ½ tsp

Garlic ½ tsp

Oil for tempering 1 tbsp

Coriander to garnish

Method

For making vadya

In a pan, heat oil. Add in mustard. Once it starts spluttering, add the curry leaves and asafoetida. Pour in the water. Let this boil. Add gram flour and mix well. To this, add chopped coriander.

Cover the pan with a plate and pour some water on top of it. This arrangement helps generate steam inside the vessel and allow quick cooking. When done, scoop out the mix and spread evenly on a greased surface. Roll it out with a greased rolling pin to about half a centimetre thickness. Once cool, cut into squares or diamond shapes.

For making aamti

Cook the dal till done. Using a spoon, mash it well and set aside.

In a pan roast onion and coconut in little oil. Once the coconut is slightly brown, cool and grind into a smooth paste. Grind ginger-garlic and coriander into a paste as well.

In a separate pan, heat oil and add cumin seeds. Once the seeds splutter, add in both ground masalas. Pour in a cup of water. Add cooked harbaraa dal. Add turmeric, red chilli powder and salt.

Once the mixture starts boiling, add the pieces of vadya.

Turn the heat off and garnish with coriander.

Enjoy with a plateful of rice or Polya. I love this Aamti with Jwari Bhakri.

Instead of adding the vadya to the cooked daal, boil the vadya in tempered and seasoned stock by adding water. Thicken the stock using a piece of vadya or even yessar pithi.

Kurdayancha Upma

Ingredients

Kurdai, 8-10

Water to boil and soak kurdai

Onion ½, chopped

Green chillies 1-2, chopped

Coriander, chopped

Peanuts (optional) a handful

Salt, sugar, lemon juice to taste

For tempering

Oil 1 tsp

Mustard seeds 1 tsp

Asafoetida a pinch

Udid dal 1 tsp

Curry leaves 8-10

Method

Boil water in a saucepan. Soak kurdai in it for a few minutes until soft. Drain the kurdai in a colander. Fluff them up slightly with a fork.

In another pan, heat oil and temper mustard seeds, asafoetida and curry leaves. Add chopped green chillies and udid dal, followed by the peanuts. Add the onions. Cook until translucent. To this, add the boiled kurdai. Mix well. Add salt to taste. Squeeze in some lemon juice and sprinkle over a pinch of sugar.

Cover and cook for two mins.

Garnish with coriander leaves before serving.

Varan Phala

Varan refers to the daal and *phala* which literally means fruits.

For this one needs three frugal resources: Varan, wheat flour dough and seasoning

For the Chich-Gulache Varan:

Ingredients

Toor dal 1 cup

Red chilli powder 1 tsp

Turmeric 1 1 tsp

Kaala Masala 2 tsp

Tamarind pulp (extracted) 1 tbs

Jaggery to balance the sweetness

Oil for tempering 1 tsp

Coriander to garnish

For the dough

Wheat flour 2 cups

Salt 1 tsp

Make a smooth dough and set aside.

Method

Cook the daal till soft. Using a spoon, mash it and set aside.

In a pan, heat oil and temper mustard seeds. Once the seeds splutter, add turmeric, red chilli powder, asafoetida and salt. Pour in a cup of water, tamarind pulp and jaggery to balance the tang. Add cooked toor daal.

Roll out polya and cut into squares, Put these into the varan. Let these dough pieces boil in varan until done. The pieces should not taste raw. Once cooked, serve this one pot meal with dollops of tup and pickle or chutney of your choice.

Haatawarchya Shevayaa

Shevai is unique hand-pulled vermicelli and make delicious milk pudding served on auspicious occasions. It is also used to make savoury upma. Shevayaanchi kheer and the recipe is mentioned in update with the new name when decided section.

Ingredients

Wheat semolina 1 cup

Clarified butter (ghee) ½ tsp

Salt to taste

Water

Method

Knead the semolina, clarified butter, salt and water into a soft, pliable dough. Cover and set aside for a couple of hours. Using a mortar and pestle, pound the mixture for at least 10 minutes. Knead the dough well on a clean surface to work up the gluten. Cover the dough with a damp cloth. Grease your palms with clarified butter. Roll a small amount of the dough first into a ball, then gradually into a thin sausage shape. Using both hands, start pulling the dough gently into long, thin strands of vermicelli; hang them on a long rod to dry (a clothes hanger works well for this). Unlike kurdai, shevayi does not have to sun dry, but avoid making it in cold and wet weather. Ajji recommends using a cylindrical steel tumbler, or *paanyache bhaande* (wrap the dough around it in thin strands and the ease off the formed shevai) to make pulling the vermicelli easier, if the traditional way seems daunting. Alternatively, a shevayi press is another convenient gadget you can use.

Once dry, store the shevai in an air-tight container.

My grandmother's tips:

1. The dough should be pliable, but not too soft. Resting it makes it better suited for hand pulling (Haatawarchya Shevayaa).

2. Too little salt will cause the shevai to break and too much will make the dough difficult to pull.

3. Wheat semolina contains more of gluten so it helps build the elasticity.

Shevayancha Upma

Ingredients

Shevaya 1 cup

Udid daal 2 tbsp

Peanuts (peas or corn works well too) 1/4 cup

Fresh coconut, ½, grated

Green chillies, 5-6, chopped

Onion, 1, chopped

Clarified butter (ghee) 1 tbsp

Coriander chopped for garnishing

Curry leaves 5-6

Salt to taste

Cumin seeds 1 tsp

Lemon juice 1 tsp

Oil for tempering 1 tbsp

Asafoetida a pinch

Method

Roast the shevaya in ghee.

Temper the cumin seeds in oil in a hot pan. Add the Udid daal, curry leaves, chopped green chillies and peanuts, followed by the chopped onions. Sauté until the onion turns translucent. If you are using peas and corns, add them now. Stir.

Add just enough water to cook the vegetables but not too much, because it can make the preparation soggy. Add the salt and lemon juice. Add the Shevaya. Cover and steam.

Garnish with coconut and coriander. This upma makes a filling breakfast and is delicious with a cup of tea.

Note: You can make Gavhalyancha Upma by substituting shevaya with gavhale.

Sugarcraft

Aparna Kulkarni

Sugar plays a significant role in the kitchen and it is a medium that allows myriad creations. It acts as a sweetener, as an additive to balance the taste in any food and definitely as a source of energy. There is more to sugar and its properties in the rename section of the book, but in this chapter, I would like to focus on the beautiful creations made from sugar. By making use of the transition stages in the making of a syrup, sugar is traditionally crafted in various ways – e.g. cast sugar artefacts, Sankranticha halwa, chikki using jaggery, Gudhi Padwyachya gaathi and Laxmi pujanache bataase

When I moved to England, I saw sugar craft used as cake decorations. Indian confectionary skills, with its heritage is an age-old tradition carried forward from mothers to daughters for generations, but is far less known and needs recognition.

Deo family is like a fabric woven intricately into loving, powerful bonds. Each part of the family lives fairly close to the others, even though it may be in a different town. When it comes to festive occasions, everyone joins in to celebrate. A smallest of celebration will involve a minimum of fifty members of the family; and when it comes to a Deo wedding, there will be at least two hundred people present, all from within the family, including a baby or two in diapers!

What amazes me about this family is the importance they place on preserving family treasures. I have watched my late mother-in-law make *vide also called as vaan* (packs of sweets) endlessly for each of the married girls during Sankranti. I believe those small gestures made the bonds even stronger between the families. The ritual also meant that the girls could connect to emotion and tradition behind the sweets and the care packages sent by their *kakus, atyas, mavshis* or *mamis*. There are so many of these rituals that are is still in focus and followed by the family. My father-in-law, who is well into his seventies, visits his sister for Raksha-Bandhan every year. My sisters-in-law try to make sure they come to their parents' home on Padwa during Diwali, to give their father the much-awaited traditional massage with *sugandhi* oil, followed by the abhyanga snaan. Such beautiful rituals find an extra dimension once everyone comes together to make them happen.

Cast sugar has long been a part of Marathi culture. Wedding ceremonies are marked by a display of the trousseau (*rukhwat*) put up by the bride's family and includes impressive edible artefacts. The artistically done sugar craft may even be made with reduced milk or shrikhandachi goli put together to form fantastic shapes. I recall my Mami's work on *khobre*, or dry coconut – she carved a *kaasav* (tortoise) or a *tabla-dagga* (a set of Indian drums)! These edible decorations took ages to create and I just loved gazing at the rukhwat table! Sugar is hygroscopic, thus when granulated sugar is sprinkled with water and mixed well, it absorbs and retains the moisture. This mixture is then packed into moulds and left to dry, allowing the water to evaporate naturally. The dried sugar attains the pattern of the cavities it is packed into. A little refinement is provided with knives or spoons used to carve the dried sugar, resulting in beautiful creations. A drop of water helps to make small holes to produce a filigree effect. Once the sculpting is done, the piece is allowed to dry. Usually, a bride's *rukhwat* displays plates and bowls carved out of sugar, along with large oil lamps, coconuts, tulsi vrundavan and a platter of goodies like modak and karanji.

I am glad my family still treasures this ritual – the bride's family puts in herculean efforts to set up a table with beautiful work handcrafted either by the bride or her aunts and cousins. This ritual probably started so that the bride could please her in-laws with the intricate work she displayed. The spread of goodies like *laadu, chivda, karanjya and anaarse* was for the young ones in the new family, who looked forward to some special treats after the wedding.

The artistically done sugar castings or those made with reduced milk and sugar and at times, *shrikhandachi goli* was another way of pleasing the little troupe at home.

The family puts together all the essentials for a bride's trousseau, including the kitchen vessels she could need in her marital home. The aunts and female cousins sit together to create the other part of the *rukhwat*: intricately embroidered or at times patch-worked bedsheets, pillow covers or a crocheted toran or a runner.

Beautiful paintings or candles made by the bride take centre stage. A *sapta padi* display is especially fascinating. It consists of the essential elements of the bride's marital jewellery, like the *mangalsutra* (bridal necklace made with black beads and gold), *jodwe* (silver toe rings) and green bangles placed along with handcrafted footsteps, with messages for the bride to lead a blissful married life.

Lagnachi pangat or the wedding scene is created with betel nuts and even shows the intricately crafted bullock cart and *palkhi*! To make the rukhwat even more elaborate, jars of dry fruits, pickles or mukhwas are dotted over the table.

The most interesting part of the preparations is the ritual of making five types of *khiri/valvat/gavhale*. Rolled with the fingers, making this is the most enjoyable part of creating *rukhwat*.

Come *Sankranti, kaateri halwa (Sankranticha halwa)* are beaded together to make beautiful ornaments like *Tanmani, Mangalsutra, Kambar patta, Bangdya* for a new bride or *Bal Krishna's* ornament for the new born in the family.

Tilachya Vadya

Sankranti is celebrated in January and always has sesame brittle or balls (*tilgul*), or *laadu* made in a Marathi kitchen. Friends and relatives share the goodies. I remember the spiked sugar beads that we distributed during the occasion. I loved munching on them as a child! Our elders have mentioned about *Til* (sesame) which provides warmth to the body during the winter, and the sugar is a symbol of the sentiment expressed during the festival: "*Tilgul ghya, goad goad bola!*" (Have tilgul and speak sweetly).

Ingredients

Sesame 1 cup
Jaggery ½ cup
Clarified butter 1 tsp

Method

In a pan roast the sesame seeds till lightly toasted and golden in colour. Grind coarsely and set aside. To the same pan, add clarified butter and jaggery. As the jaggery begins to melt, stir carefully – the molten syrup can give you a nasty burn! It behaves in the same way as sugar syrup does when heated. Just before it reaches a firm ball stage, turn the heat off and mix in the coarsely ground sesame seeds. Spread evenly on a greased plate or tray and let it set. Using a greased knife, cut through the *chikki* to make little squares. Once it cools down, break apart the brittle.

To make *laadu*, roll the sesame-jaggery mix into balls. This needs to be done as quickly as possible, before the mix cools and hardens. I have seen women wetting their palms with cold water before rolling *laadu* or even greasing their palms with clarified butter to protect their palms from being burned.

Sankranticha Halwa

One Christmas holiday, I was watching a BBC documentary on English confectionary through the ages. To my amazement, I found confits (sugar-coated caraway seeds), sugar plums (with almonds as the centre) and ragged confits or bandstrings (slivered cinnamon dipped in sugar syrup) as the oldest forms of sugar confectionary in Europe. Caraway confits were consumed at the end of a meal with spiced wines, as a carminative. Sugar plums survived into modern times as sugared almonds. There is also evidence of smooth confits made with low density sugar syrups, while those with a ragged or rougher appearance were made with a thicker syrup. A pearling funnel helped express a steady stream of sugar syrup into a warm pan swirled over the stove – the beads were rubbed with the hands to separate them. I find these sharing similarity to sugar confectionary in Marathi cuisine too.

Traditional Marathi cuisine boasts of *Badishep Golya* (smooth confits in the West) and *Sankranticha Kaateri Halwa* (the rough or ragged version of the confit).

My mother-in-law suggested using a brass paraat (her mother-in-law always used a brass paraat) to make the sugar beads. It is a tedious task, for sure, but worth it.

For this, you need the following utensils: brass paraat (a flat vessel), iron tawa and heat-resistant fingers. Yes, the stirring is done by hands and not with spoons. More practically, a silicon brush works wonders!

Sankranticha Halwa

Ingredients

1. You may use puffed rice, sesame seeds, flattened rice, pumpkin seeds, candy sugar, fennel seeds and other such tiny particles to 'seed' the sugar syrup to form a coat. Ultra-thin coats of sugar will encapsulate a fine particle of any of these seeds used, creating unique spiky beads. Ideally use 1 teaspoon of any of the ingredients mentioned above. I find sesame seeds easier to work with.

2. To make sugar syrup I used caster sugar from my pantry. To this, one may use gel food colour, which is optional.

To make the sugar syrup

Sugar 1 cup

Water 2 + 1.5 cups

Yogurt 1 tsp

Milk ¼ cup

Sesame seeds 1 tsp

Method

Soak a cup of sugar in water twice the quantity of water for about 10-15 mins. To this, add a teaspoon of yogurt.

Add 1.5 cups of water additionally and place sugar-water-yogurt mix on the heat. Make sure the heat is kept low. Add milk one teaspoon at a time, which will help in getting rid of the scum the sugar carries. Strain this off using a clean muslin cloth. Place the strained syrup back on the heat. Repeat this process 2-3 times, adding milk each time and straining off the scum until the syrup is clean and clear.

Boil the syrup to one-thread consistency. It should neither be too thin nor too thick.

Traditionally, a *shegdi/choolah* (a traditional stove fuelled by coal and wood) is used to make *halwa*. Once the fire is burning consistently, there is an even distribution of heat, facilitating the spikes to form on the catalyst used.

To make these sugar beads, we need an assembly of an iron *tawa* (pan) with a brass *paraat* atop. This whole assembly is placed on the heat.

PAAT PAANI

Place a teaspoon of sesame seeds or puffed rice or any other catalyst of your choice into the brass *paraat*.

A teaspoon of sesame seeds yields around half a cups of *tilgul*. Make sure the gas is burning entirely on low heat. One needs to add a drop sugar syrup every minute onto the sesame seeds and stir delicately with fingers. Be cautious as it will burn your hands, so it is a rather challenging process. I found that using a silicone brush made it easier and less painful!

Continue the process of pouring sugar syrup and stirring. It is a long wait, and you need to be patient till you start seeing spikes. I did it for an hour in the morning and an hour in the evening. It was only the next day that after another hour of coating and stirring that I could see spikes appearing. Carry on the layering and stirring until you are happy with the size of the *tilgul*.

Each of the particles is coated with the sugar syrup to create the intricate spikes. Make sure not to add more syrup or else the *kaata* (spikes) will dissolve in the molten sugar.

Once done, let the sugar beads cool and store them in an air-tight container.

Notes:

1. Always keep the heat at the lowest setting. Brass pans set on a *tava* are best, since steel vessels overheat.

2. If the brass *paraat*/vessel starts getting a sugar syrup coating, it may break the spikes created on the seeds. Place the beads on a separate plate. Wash the brass plate and dry it well before continuing the process.

3. Do not rush the stirring. Stir delicately. I used the silicone baking brush only after making sure that it was not breaking the spikes.

4. If the weather is hot, do this in the early hours of the day and the evening – it is sweaty work!

5. Have patience and do not rush the process. I needed three days to get the results I wanted.

6. Enjoy the whole process – it is oddly therapeutic.

Battaase

These sugar nuggets are offered to Goddess Laxmi during Diwali.

Ingredients

Sugar 1/2 cup

Water less than a 1/4 cup

Baking soda ¼ tsp

Method

Stir the sugar and water together and let it simmer for 5 min in a pan. Once the syrup starts thickening, add food colour of your choice. I added gel food colour. Stir continuously. Turn off the heat. Add 1/4 tsp baking soda and mix well.

Drop spoonfuls of syrup onto a non-stick, heat-proof surface. Leave aside to cool and harden.

Gaathi

To make *Gaathi*, you need several moulds of the same shape. Ideally, a silicone baking or a chocolate making mould comes in handy to make this. You need the same sugar syrup used for *battaase*. Using the same ingredients mentioned above for *battaase*, one can make two small lengths of sugar garlands.

Set the moulds in a straight line. Place a long piece of string along the row, over each of the shapes, before pouring in the syrup and letting it set. Make sure that the string is in place, across the middle of each mould and dipping halfway into the sugar syrup. Once cold and hardened, release from the moulds carefully. You should have a long line of sugar drops on a string!

Mukhwaas

Ladies rolling Papad

The Attic Door

My paternal aunts, uncle, parents, sister and cousins gathered at our Ambejogai *wada* every summer to spend time with Tai and Babu, my grandparents. Kaka, my uncle, was as mischievous as any young lad at the age of 15-16 years could be, with his nieces and nephews. He played marbles with us in the *gotha* (cow barn) that was next to the *wada*. Every morning we climbed up on the tinned roof of the *gotha* and Kaka would break twigs of neem from the branch that covered the roof to clean our teeth. The bitter taste we got from chewing the twigs – that is how to brush teeth with fresh neem! – was just awful, but it was the morning ritual!

The elders spent their afternoons chatting in the courtyard, while we played *bhatukli* on the stairs. Puffed rice, peanuts and jaggery made the meals for our games. At times *atya* would send us on errands.

A small lane led to a temple and it ended at the market. I loved roaming through the market with my cousins, buying colourful bangles and *tiklya* (*bindi*). One time, I remember, my cousin Shilpa and I managed to take our piggy bank to the temple. We saw a few people at the temple dropping money in the *daan peti* (charity box). I looked at Shilpa and saw that she was thinking the same thing I was. We went into the temple, bowed to the idol, did a *pradakshina* (round) and dropped a coin from our piggy bank into the box. I wished for a goodie and a toy. What fun, I thought, Let's do that again! Shilpa liked the idea. Around we went for the next *pradakshina* followed by a wish and another coin dropped in the *peti*. We checked the piggy bank. It had loads of coins. So we went around again and again until the money was all gone. Both of us were so chuffed, because we were anticipating our wishes being granted. We trotted back to our *wada* and gleefully narrated the whole incident to my *atya*. What chaos she created in the house! This was not the reaction we had expected. We were escorted to the temple and my *atya* asked to speak to the priest about the incident. Why would a temple priest give back money from the *daan peti*? Atya and we scampered back to the *wada*. Up we went to the massive *maadi* (attic), where Babu (grandfather) had his study. It had a *kothi* (storage for kitchen essentials), and the walls had ropes tied from one end to the other for the laundry to dry. One of the walls had a small door, only slightly bigger than a window. No wonder then that it was referred to as *lahaan daar* (small door)! It reminded me of the small door Alice had to walk through during her adventures in Wonderland. This little door was different though – it opened on to the tin roof of the next *gotha*. The other wall extended into Babu's small room. He was a writer and spent hours there working on his books. All I recall of what happened next is a smile on his face and his long index finger upraised and his whisper: "*Labaadi keli na?*" (been mischievous?). Babu did not tell us off. In fact, once the women calmed down, he called us to him and started narrating us a story!

I wish I could go back in time, just to peek into that *maadi* one more time or sit next to Babu!

Bhatukli food

Peanut-jaggery laadu and Chigul

We made these every year on our visit to Aurangabad during the school holidays. *Khel paani* (role-playing kitchen activities) was a ritual in the afternoon when the grandparents were resting. This was the time when mother and her sisters were busy with extra jobs like washing their gold jewellery and sari with soapnuts or even starching cotton sari using sabudana starch. Mami would join us siblings and cousins making *Chigul* lollipops, peanut-jaggery *laadu* (by splitting a peanut and stuffing it with jaggery) and *churmure*!

Chigul is made with tart tamarind, jaggery, red chilli powder and salt. These are pounded together and rolled into tiny balls to make our favourite childhood substitute for candies.

Mukhwaas

Akka *aaji*, my mother's *atya*, would spend summer afternoons entertaining the little ones with her skills. I recall her making different types of *vide* with betelnut leaves. It was amazing to watch her fingers move and twist the leaves into different shapes. I can just about make a *Govind vida*, which I learned because it had my father's name. Those afternoons were spent mostly sharing ideas and experiences until *nashtyachi vel* (tea time). If a wedding was around the corner, a *yaadi* of *masale*, chutney, pickles and other must-makes would be put together with *mukhshudhi* and *supari* as essential components.

My husband's aunt, Kamal *kaku* makes sure each of the women, young or old, gets a *vida* made with love and care after all the hardships in the kitchen during a *kulaachar*. To make *Tambul*, she would crush *vida* in a small brass *khal-batta* and treat the ladies.

Every household keeps a seed mix in a jar as a mouth freshener. Sangeeta *mavshi* suggests "*Til, baalantshepa, owa, jawas ani badishep bhajun thevavi ani roj ek chamcha chaavun khaane.*" Sesame, dill, carom, flax and fennel seeds contain essential oils. Chewing this lightly roasted combination every day is a norm to aid digestion.

Khaareek Paachak Supaari

Ingredients

Dried dates 250 g

Lemon juice 2 cups

Black salt 1 tsp

Method

Chop the dates into 2-3 pieces and soak in lemon juice for 3 days. The dates plump up. Chop these further into tiny pieces and place them in a plate. Sprinkle with black salt, mix well and sun dry.

Store in an airtight container.

. . . .

Aawlyache Paachak

Ingredients

Indian gooseberries 6, washed and grated

Ginger 1/4 cup, grated

Cumin powder 1 tbs

Salt 1 tbs

Method

Mix grated gooseberries and ginger. Sprinkle with cumin powder and salt and spread on a plate. Sun dry and store in an air-tight container.

Taambul

Ingredients

Betelnut leaves 25

Kaat (Catechu) (optional)

Cloves 15

Green cardamoms 10

Carom seeds 2 tsp

Liquorice powder 2 tsp

Dhana daal (roasted

coriander seeds) 2 tsp

Khadi saakhar (sugar candy) 1tsp

Fennel seeds 4 tbs

Method

Soak the leaves in water for 5 mins. Wipe and dry. Smear *kaath* – just a dot – on each leaf. Cover and set the leaves aside. Shell the cardamom pods. Chop the leaves into small portions. Grind together with rest of the ingredients. If the leaves are well soaked, they get nicely ground. Store in an air-tight container. You could add 1 tsp of *Gulkand* to add sweetness.

. . . .

Bina Supariche Mukhwaas

Ingredients

Fennel seeds 2 cups

Grated dry coconut 1 cup

Caraway seeds ½ cup

Carom seeds ¼ cup

Cloves 10

Green cardamom 10

Mace 2

Liquorice powder 1 tsp

Black salt 1/4 tsp

Salt 1/4 tsp

Method

Except for black salt and salt, dry roast each of the ingredients. Add salts and grind to a fine powder.

Glossary

A
Aleev – Garden cress
Ale – Ginger
Ambe halad – Mango ginger
Amba – Ripe mango
Amsul – Garcinia fruit skin, Kokum
Ambaadi – Sorrels
Awala – Indian gooseberries

B
Badishep – fennel seeds
Barni – a ceramic jar
Bataata – potatoes
Baajri – pearl millet
Baalantshepa – Dill seeds
Bhagar – Samo seeds
Bharad – coarsely ground
Bhokra – Gumberries

C
Chakka – strained yogurt
Chinch – Tamarind
Churmure – puffed rice
Chul – clay oven

D
Dabba – container traditionally made of steel or brass
Daale – split roasted gram
Daane – Peanuts
Daaliche peeth – Gramflour, chickpea flour
Dagad phool – Black stone flower (lichens)
Dahi – Yogurt, curds
Dhane – Coriander seeds

Dhanaa daal – roasted coriander seeds
Dhabbu mirchi – capsicum, green pepper
Dink – edible gum
Dodke – Ridge gourd
Doodh – milk
Dudhi – Bottlegourd

F
Farsaan – crisp, savoury mix topped on misal

G
Ganpati – Elephant God
Gaajar – Carrots
Gahu – Wheat
Gavaar – Cluster beans
Godache/goadache padaarth – desserts
Gul – Jaggery
Gulkand – rose petals conserve

H
Halad – turmeric
Harbaraa daal – Split chickpea
Hing – asafoetida
Hirve tomato – green tomatoes
Hirvi mirchi – green chillies

J
Jawas – Flaxseeds
Jeere – cumin seeds
Jeshthamadh – Liquorice
Jwari – Sorghum flour

K
Kadhai – Deep pan

GLOSSARY

Kaat – catechu

Kaaral – Niger seeds

Kaakdi – Cucumber

Kaalvan – accompaniments to pair with breads or rice

Kanda – Onion

Kadhi limbachi paane, kadhi paala, kadhi patta – Curry leaves

Kairi – Raw mango

Kaali miri – Black pepper

Kanik – whole wheat flour

Karle – bitter gourds

Kaju – Cashews

Kavath – Wood apple

Keshar – Saffron

Khobra(sukka) – dry coconut

Khaanaawal – a small eatery serving homemade meals

Khamang – piquant

Khareek – dried dates

Khaar/lonche khaar – pickle masala from a matured pickle

Khus khus – Poppy seeds

Khadi saakhar – Sugar candy

Khapli gahu – Emmer wheat

Khal batta – traditional mortar and pestle

Khawa – Milk solids

Khudleli/khudun – bruised through tearing leaves

Kothimbir – fresh coriander leaves

Krushna/Krishna – Lord Krishna

L

Lal tikhat – Red chilli powder

Lasun – Garlic

Limbu – Lemon

M

Maida – Plain four

Maeenmula – Coleus roots

Methi – fenugreek seeds

Methi paala – Fenugreek leaves

Mohri – Mustard seeds

Moog daal – split green gram

Mohor – flowers

Meeth – Salt

Mula – Radish

N

Naaral – Fresh coconut

O

Oli Halad – raw turmeric

Owa – carom seeds

P

Paat Paani – setting the meal

Paat – short wooden seat

Paata – varvanta – traditional grinding stone

Pangat – rows of seating arrangement for meals

Pandhra – white

Paraat – a wide, shallow plate for kneaded flour

Paale bhajya – leafy vegetables

Pela/pele – traditional tumbler to drink water from

Phal bhajya – vegetable fruits that are fleshy and have seeds

Phodni – tempering

Phutane – roasted Bengal gram

Phule – flowers

Pohe – pounded/flattened rice

Pithi saakhar – powdered sugar

R

Rangoli – patterns adorned on the floor using white powder

Rawa – Semolina

Rataale – sweet potatoes

Rajgira – Amaranth seeds

S
Sapeeth/sapith – very fine
Saakhar – Sugar
Saaran (often called puran) – savoury or sweet filling
Sabudana – Sago seeds
Shepu/shepu paala – Dill leaves
Sorya – kitchen press with a variety of attachments to press through
Sukya lal mirchya – dry red chillies

T
Taat – Traditional plate to serve meals on
Taandul – rice
Taambda – red
Taambya – traditional vessel(jug) to fill water

Taak – Buttermilk
Tel – oil
Til – Sesame seeds
Tur daal – Split pigeon pea
Tup – clarified butter

U
Udid daal – split blackgram

V
Vaangi – Aubergines
Vaatya – traditional bowls to serve vegetables, daals and desserts
Veldode – Cardamom pods
Vidyachi paane – betelnut leaves

W
Waalke – Yellow cucumber, Madras kaakdi

Printed in Great Britain
by Amazon